The Second Promise

Eddie's Remarkable Journey to Redemption

The Second Promise
Eddie's Remarkable
Journey To Redemption

Gary Edward Hopkins

Phone: (507) 269-6327
Email: gehopkins9@gmail.com
Available at Amazon, Barnes and Noble & iTunes

Gary Edward Hopkins

ISBN 978-1-0980-9756-1 (paperback)
ISBN 978-1-0980-9758-5 (hardcover)
ISBN 978-1-0980-9757-8 (digital)

Christian Faith Publishing, Inc.
832 Park Avenue
Meadville, PA 16335
www.christianfaithpublishing.com

Unless otherwise noted, all scripture references are from KJV

Printed in the United States of America

Introduction

The story you are about to read is true. The events of my father's life were told to me by my two uncles who knew him well and by my father. I am writing this book to give hope to believers concerning their unsaved loved ones and to encourage and bring hope to those who are bound by addiction, especially alcohol.

To those who are addicted to alcohol, there is hope for a new life free from the deadly grip of alcoholism. Never give up hope. You are not a hopeless alcoholic, not to the one who created you and not to me. Remember, you are beautifully and wonderfully made by your creator. You do not have a hopeless future without a chance of redemption and freedom from addiction.

Part 2 of this book will instruct believers how to pray for the deliverance and salvation of their loved ones suffering with addiction according to the Word of God. The revelation of how to pray for the lost must not die with me. I cannot keep silent knowing what I know. This is my father's life story and his testimony of redemption.

Read it and be blessed.

Part One

As a child, my father experienced rejection, abuse, neglect, and lone-liness, which slowly turned into anger and resentment. By the time Eddie Hopkins was in his twenties, he had more layers of hurt and anger than a large white onion. Many pastors, including his beloved grandmother Elizabeth Pease, who was a Bible-teaching, born-again believer, attempted to peel off those layers of anger, but to no avail. After several decades of watching my father reject the gospel and sink lower into despair, there were believers who stated, "If ever there was a 'hopeless case' spiritually, it is surely Eddie Hopkins." But these naysayers did not know that Dad had a praying grandmother who knew how to pray and intercede for the lost. Grandma Pease, through intercessory prayer, built a hedge of protection encircling my father's life so that he would not be destroyed by his dangerous and reckless behavior until he could have an encounter with Jesus Christ.

My father's life was filled with drama, danger, and dozens of near-death experiences. Could it be that his grandmother's prayers to sustain and protect him until he could hear Jesus whisper his name were answered? Or was it just good old luck that kept him alive all those crazy years?

My father was born and grew up near Webster City, Iowa, and later lived in the Clear Lake, Iowa, area. His childhood was filled with physical and mental abuse. Unfortunately, Dad was born with a speech impediment that caused him to talk as though he was retarded. His mother was embarrassed by Dad's disability and would hide him in a closet, in total darkness, whenever friends would visit. There were times when he would even end up wetting himself. As a child, he was often whipped with a long-handled screwdriver and slapped for minor infractions.

My dad experienced a miracle during a doctor's visit when he was nine years old. The doctor noted my dad's odd speech and performed an oral exam. Dad was diagnosed with ankyloglossia, or in layman's terms, he was tongue-tied. This is a condition in which an unusually short or tight band of tissue tethers the bottom of the tongue's tip to the floor of the mouth. The doctor then performed minor surgery in his office, and suddenly, Dad was no longer disabled or "retarded." Dad was no longer a closet case, but the emotional damage was already done. Dad grew up feeling that he was of no value, feeling worthless, and looking at a hopeless future.

When he was about thirteen years old, he met a young man named Dick Murphy. Dad and Dick had something in common; they both were from abusive and neglectful homes. Together they formed a tight bond of friendship, and together they formed a "third personality" that led them into dangerous situations and destructive behavior. But more on their wild and crazy life later.

Dad was in eighth grade, and school was almost out for the summer break. Dad was most likely goofing off in class when the teacher told him to follow her into a large closet where she was going to whip him. At that moment, Dad decided that he had spent enough time in closets and that no adult was going to ever abuse him again. He quickly ran to the window and climbed out on the ledge. He was on the second floor of the school building. In those days, sewer pipes were made of clay and were connected to the outside of the building walls. Like a monkey, Dad shimmied down the clay pipes until he was safely on the ground. He sprinted across a field to the railroad tracks and hopped on a freight train that was headed east. He had just turned fourteen years old and had no idea how he would survive or where he was going when he climbed into that box car. To his surprise there were several black men (hobos) riding that train. At first, he was alarmed for he had never been around African Americans and he wasn't sure how they would treat him. But instead of harming him, for the next three months, they protected him and taught him how to scavenge for food that was fit to eat. They gave him clothes (that didn't fit), and his black protectors taught him how to cook on an open fire and make delicious mulligan stew.

While riding the freight trains that summer, Dad developed a love for black people that stayed with him for the rest of his life. Those black men became the first adults Dad ever trusted. Was it luck that helped Dad survive three months riding freight trains, or was it Grandma's prayers?

As a side note, when Dad turned fifty-two, he moved to South Central Los Angeles, which was predominantly a black community. He wanted to be close to black people and to be where he could hang out, play cards, and drink with them. He found black people funny and witty, and they laughed at his jokes and treated him like family. While I was growing up, Dad never allowed the N-word to be spoken in our home.

At the end of that summer, Dad returned home to Clear Lake; and this time, there were no whippings or physical abuse. His parents knew if they whipped or punished him for running away, he would simply disappear again.

When Dad returned home, after being a "hobo," he quickly hooked up with his friend Dick Murphy, and they continued their shenanigans, occasionally getting into trouble for trespassing on property or committing minor offenses.

Dad and his friends enjoyed playing tricks on people. One of their favorite pranks was to overturn outhouses located in people's backyards. Outhouses were toilets made of wood that set over a large hole that had been dug in the ground. Outhouses were usually placed about twenty-five meters behind a home. One night, during Halloween, Dad, Dick, and another friend were attempting to tip over an outhouse. It had been raining, the grass was slippery, and disaster struck. As the boys tipped over the outhouse, poetic justice happened. As the outhouse fell over, their friend slipped on the wet grass and fell headfirst into the hole with human waste. Dad and Dick would not let their friend get near them. In fact, they ran away from him as fast as they could. Can you imagine the horror his parents experienced when their son showed up at the front door covered in human defecation?

During 1930, Dad and Dick turned fifteen years old. By this time, they both had been introduced to alcohol and were frequent users. Prohibition was still the law, and all sales and distribution of alcohol were prohibited. Dad never shared how or where he and his friend procured their supply of alcohol at that young age.

One evening, Dad and his friend were riding their bikes outside of town when they saw a vehicle driving down a dirt road into the woods with its lights off. The two stopped riding their bikes and watched two men get out of their vehicle and bury something among the trees. The boys thought the men were burying a dead body. They waited for the men to leave, and with excitement, they hurried to what they thought was a grave. With their hands, they began digging into the loose dirt and soon discovered a cache of liquor. They took a couple of bottles and headed to Dick's house to hide their stash and to sample their newly acquired alcohol. They were sixteen years old.

A few days later, they returned to the buried "treasure" to retrieve more bottles of booze. They soon returned again to steal more hidden liquor. Only this time, two gangsters were lying in wait for them. The gangsters had them kneel, and they put pistols to the back of their heads. Dad said he knew he was going to die and waited for the sudden impact of the bullet. Then to the boy's surprise and delight, one of the gangsters gave them a choice to either work for them or die on the spot. Of course, the two wisely chose the first offer and immediately started a new career—smuggling illegal liquor throughout Missouri and Iowa for the mob—at the age of seventeen. It's important to note that Dad and Dick did not work full-time for the mob. They were slowly introduced to the world of smuggling and were "on call" for the mob whenever a load of liquor needed to be transported. Miraculously, Dad did not die that night at the hands of the mobsters. Maybe he was just lucky, or was his survival because of his grandma's intercessory prayers?

Dad worked part-time transporting illegal liquor in Iowa and across state lines for several years. Prohibition ended on December 5, 1933, but bootlegging liquor in Iowa remained illegal. Iowa remained a dry state after prohibition was abolished.

One night, Dad was driving around Mason City with a stolen vehicle full of illegal liquor. His contact person was not at the designated location where he was to deliver the booze. Suddenly, the car behind him lit up with flashing lights. It was the police, and Dad decided to outrun them. He drove through stop signs and up and down alleys, and finally, he bailed out of the car and ran through backyards and over fences until he saw a church. It was Wednesday evening, and the church was open for services. Dad ran up to the front door, entered the church, sat between parishioners, lifted his hands, worshipped the Lord, and clapped his hands to the music like the others. He heard the church door behind him open and dared not look back. He knew it was the police. He stayed until the service ended and asked someone for a ride home. Dad was eighteen years old, and if he had been caught and sentenced for car theft and bootlegging liquor, he could have spent ten years in federal prison. I guess he was just lucky, or was Grandma Elizabeth's prayers following him? "The effectual fervent prayer of a righteous man availeth much" (James 5:16). Incidentally, if Dad would have been caught and sent to prison, I would not be here writing this story.

My grandfather Milton, my dad's father, owned an auto repair shop and sold used Hudson cars in Woolstock, Iowa. It was winter when Dad, without permission, took one of the Hudsons on a joyride. After picking up a friend and a bottle of booze, they headed for Clear Lake, Iowa, at high speed. Dad was driving on a narrow, two-lane road that followed the lakeshore when he lost control of the car (he was drunk) and hit a tree at high speed. When emergency crews arrived, they saw my Dad walking on the frozen lake, about two hundred meters offshore, slowly removing his clothing. He had incurred a severe concussion and was knocked senseless. He and his friend lived, but with serious injuries. Dad's friend was horribly disfigured. Once again, I guess Dad was just lucky, or was it…?

It is important to mention that three generations lived in my dad's home—his grandparents, parents, and his siblings. During Dad's teenage years, he would often come home late at night, and guess who would be waiting up for him—Grandma Elizabeth. Grandma would be in her rocking chair and have him kneel beside her. She would put her hand on his head and pray for his safety and that someday he would accept Jesus Christ as his personal Savior. Oh, that there were more grandmas in this world like Elizabeth Pease.

Dad was a terrific athlete; even in his forties, he was as quick as a panther. My father had a God-given athletic physique. He looked like a Greek statue when he was young. Dad was one of the bravest men I have ever known. He loathed bullies and child abusers. He spent his adult life defending people who could not defend or protect themselves. Because of his athletic ability, a trainer convinced him to go into wrestling. Dad was trained, and within a year, he had his first professional wrestling match. He was paid ten to fifteen dollars per match. The minimum wage in 1935 averaged about twelve dollars per week for a male laborer. Dad could make that much money in a fifteen-minute wrestling match.

By the time Dad was twenty years old, he was drinking heavily daily; and in spite of this, his wrestling career was taking off. He was undefeated until that fateful day. Dad and his wrestling partner were performing an unpaid exhibition match before a high school student body. They were performing a wrestling stunt when something went wrong. When Dad came down hard on the wrestling floor, he broke a vertebra in his neck. He spent the next six months in a body cast. Dad never admitted that he was liquored up when performing that day, but I believe he had been drinking heavily. His alcoholism took him away from jobs, a promising wrestling career, and eventually his family.

During those six months in a body cast, his friend Dick Murphy made sure Dad had plenty of alcohol to drink. Dad told me that he did not have much recall of those six months in a cast. During that time he stayed medicated with vodka. It was during those six months of recovery when he became a "sold-out" alcoholic. Vodka became Dad's drink of choice, rarely ever drinking another type of hard liquor.

I want you readers to know that it is not my intention to glamorize my father's reckless and dangerous behavior. It's important to know that it was his emotional pain and anger resulting from his childhood and the loss of his wrestling career that caused him to act out the way he did.

After Dad healed from the neck injury, the wrestling organization would not allow him to ever wrestle again. So his fighting arena became bars and nightclubs. I mentioned earlier that he loathed bullies and child abusers. Even though he wasn't nurtured and loved as a child, but was abused, he would defend those who couldn't protect themselves. He and Murphy spent several nights a week in bars having a good time. When a bully would appear in a bar, looking for trouble, and Dad would see him threatening someone, Dad would go up to him and intentionally bump into him. The bully would turn around, curse my dad, and grab him; and Dad would quickly dispatch the bully to the floor in pain. Dad would return to his table and finish his beer.

Dad was always looking for an opportunity to help someone or to "tune-up" a bully. One day, while Dad was at a petrol station filling up his car with gas, he heard a woman screaming and saw her trying to push a man away. The man was slapping and shoving the woman. Dad ran over to the man and grabbed him from behind and took the attacker to the ground. While Dad was holding the man on the ground, someone started hitting and kicking him. Dad looked up, and guess what? The woman he was trying to help was kicking him and screaming, "Get off my husband! Who do you think you are?" The woman's reaction to being helped seemed contrary to what Dad had expected. Dad saw the irony in the situation and decided not to get into the middle of a domestic problem again.

At the age of twelve, I started working with Dad during the summer months, painting houses and occasionally churches. They are the best memories I have with him. He was full of wisdom and proverbs. Unfortunately, alcoholism kept him from applying and walking in his own words of wisdom. He had a gift of discernment. He could meet a person and, in minutes, could tell you about their character and if you could trust them and if they would be a loyal friend. Dad could read body language and tell what kind of emotional hang-ups (problems) a person may have.

One of Dad's proverbs went like this, "Never ever make a promise to someone that you cannot or won't keep." He continued to share his words of wisdom concerning character by stating, "Remember, your word is your bond, and your handshake is your contract. Gary, when your life is over, you want people to remember you as a faithful and loyal friend, a person that kept his word, and a friend that was always there for them. This is more important than being remembered for money and fame."

Okay, I got ahead of the story. In 1938, Mom and Dad met, and the hormones took off. My mother was a beautiful Irish lady, and Dad was a man of the world—handsome, strong, and protective. Mom was only eighteen years old when she and Dad eloped. Little did she know what the next thirty years would hold. Oh! Remember earlier in the story that Dad had been working with the mob since he was seventeen years old. Now Dad had a problem: he wanted to get out of the bootlegging business. I believe Dad really loved my mother and thought he could change and start a new life. He went to the mob boss in Clear Lake, Iowa, and asked to be released from the crime family. Dad told the boss that he had met a beautiful Christian girl, that they had eloped, and that he wanted to have a new life with her. What happened next rarely ever happens in a crime family. The boss told Dad that he was free to go and gave him his blessing. Ponder for a moment what had just happened! The only way a person could leave a crime family was in a body bag. The mob boss must have really liked my dad, I guess, or was it Grandma's prayers that spared him?

Dad did a good job hiding his alcoholism and troubled past from my mom during their brief courtship and for several weeks after their marriage. When Mom discovered his serious drinking problem, she was heartbroken. She felt deceived and betrayed because she had been. She must have asked herself, "Who really is this man?" Mom had married against her family's wishes, and she had too much pride to leave Dad and return home. So she stuck it out for thirty years. It turned out to be a nightmare for both of them. I sincerely believe that Dad wanted to change and love his wife, but alcoholism had a deadly grip on his life. And though he was physically powerful, he could not break the chains of addiction. Only one person could do that. Dad would meet him in 1972.

While growing up, smoke and fire rarely cleared out of our home. When Dad was home, there was constant environmental noise. Every day, my mother had the same reaction to Dad's drinking. She would yell and scream at my dad until she nearly collapsed from exhaustion. I always thought that my mother would have made a good travel agent; she was always sending my dad on a guilt trip. For thirty years of marriage, my mother's approach and method was the same—crying and yelling—trying to get Dad to stop drinking alcohol. Friends, if you use the same method attempting to change a person's behavior for years and it hasn't worked, please consider a different approach. Here's a novel idea—love, affection, and prayer. My mother had actually taken over where Dad's mother stopped. The rejection, yelling, and name-calling continued toward Dad throughout their marriage. In defense of my mom, she was deceived when Dad hid his alcoholism and his troubled past from her.

When I was ten years old and while mowing a friend's lawn, I saw something fly into the trees and tumble through the branches to the ground. It was a sparrow hawk, and it started to flop around trying to fly. But he had broken his wing. The accident happened because the hawk was trying to get away from a swarm of wrens (small birds) that were defending their nests, and the hawk flew into a tree attempting to avoid its pursuers. I put the injured hawk in a box and took him home.

My dad had a wonderful way with animals, and throughout his life, he had rescued wild animals and was able to not only tame them but also train them. His love for defending those who couldn't protect themselves was carried over to injured animals. Dad opened the box, and the hawk jumped out and tried to fly but crashed to the floor. With a calm and gentle approach, Dad had that hawk perched on his bare forearm within thirty minutes. We named the hawk Tuffy, and he became a family pet that we all enjoyed for several years.

There were occasions when Dad brought home other strays—people. He was an interesting dichotomy. Dad had two sides to his personality that were completely opposite of the other. Hold a coin in your hand; there are two different sides, yet they are part of the same coin. He had compassion for those who were hurting and down on their luck and, with a soft voice, would help and encourage them. There were days when he gave what little he had to people in need, even if it deprived our family. By giving and helping others, Dad was doing the work of Jesus without even realizing it.

Friends, it doesn't matter if you are Christian, Jewish, or Muslim. If you are feeding the hungry, clothing the poor, and protecting the weak, you are doing the work of Jesus Christ and you are following his commandment to take care of the poor, the orphans, and the widows.

I share this next story so you will understand the level of pain and anger that possessed my dad as a result of the abuse and rejection he endured as a child.

Dad's elder sister Alma was in her home upstairs when she heard someone slowly walking up the stairs. It was at night, and the light in the room was dim. At first, she wasn't sure if it was her husband or her brother Eddie who had been doing some painting and repairs in her home earlier that day. Slowly, the shadowy figure walked toward her. As he came into the light, Alma saw that the figure was her brother. Alma told me that he was mumbling as he approached her. When he came into full view, she said his face was beet red, he had a hollow, darkened look in his eyes, and the expression on his face was one of rage. Dad thought that his sister Alma was his mother. Dad began to curse and use foul words and said, "Someone should kill you. You don't deserve to live." He was as drunk as a person can get without blacking out. Alma calmly spoke to Dad and said, "Eddie, I'm not your mother. It's Alma. Mom is not here; I am your sister." Alma told me that Dad just stood in front of her, glaring at her, which was frightening. Finally, he turned and staggered to a sofa and collapsed. Dad's heavy drinking of vodka that night brought the rage and hurt that he had been carrying all his life to the surface. Alma told me, with a heavy heart, "I don't know why mom was so cruel to your dad. I just don't know why."

I mentioned earlier that we had a pet hawk named Tuffy that we kept in a cage in our detached garage. One day as I entered the garage to feed him, I saw something that has haunted me to this day. Dad was sitting on the bottom step of a ladder, smoking a cigarette. Above him was a rope he had tied to a beam, and at the end of the rope, he had fashioned a noose. He was about to hang himself. At first, I was horrified; but with a calm voice, I began to talk him out of ending his life. I then said, "Dad, the wrestling show is about to start on television. Will you come in the house and watch it with me?" I was fourteen years old. He took a deep breath and finally said yes. I then asked him, "Do you promise?" He looked up at me and, after a long pause, said, "I promise." It is important to note that my dad was principled in certain areas. He had instructed me, as a young man, with many philosophies. One was, "Never, ever, make a promise to someone that you cannot or won't keep." I went back to the house not knowing if my dad was going to walk through the door. To my great relief, within a few minutes, he came into the house, and we watched wrestling together. We never spoke of that event again. When Dad promised to come into the house and not end his life, it was the first time he had ever made a promise to me in fourteen years, and true to his word, he kept that promise. I guess it was just a coincidence that I went to the garage to see my hawk just as Dad was about to hang himself, or was it?

A few days later, I was taking the trash to the burn barrel in the backyard when I suddenly heard a pistol shot. I froze in fear, and then I heard two more shots in succession coming from inside our house. Instead of running away from the gunfire, I ran toward it. For years, we had a .22 calibre revolver, and I knew the report of that pistol very well. As I sprinted toward the front door, I was tormented by the thought that Dad had just shot my mom and two sisters. When I dashed through the front door, Mom was holding the pistol, standing in front of Dad, and he was sitting in his easy chair. I then thought, after twenty plus years of marriage, Mom had had enough of his drinking and decided to take care of the problem. I looked for blood, but all I saw was that the dark skin of my Native American father had turned pale.

Once again, Dad had attempted suicide. While he was alone in the living room, Dad put the pistol under his chin while he was smoking a cigarette. His hand was shaking so badly that when the pistol discharged, the first bullet went straight up toward the ceiling, striking the cigarette and sending pieces of tobacco into the air. Dad still had what was remaining of that cigarette in his mouth. It was one of the most bizarre scenes I have ever witnessed—Dad sitting in his chair with the stub of a cigarette in his mouth, Mom standing in front of him with a pistol in her hand, pieces of cigarette paper and tobacco floating down from the ceiling, the smell of gun powder, and Dad and Mom staring at each other with both of their faces as white as sheets.

I took the gun away from Mom and screamed, "What's going on!" This is what happened. Dad fired the first shot, missing his chin by about an inch. Mom ran into the living room, grabbed the gun, and fired two more bullets into the floor. Mom never explained why she did that. While lying in bed later that night, I remember laughing at the devil and saying, "You had two chances to destroy my dad this week, and you couldn't do it!" I wonder what force was really shaking my dad's hand so violently when he pulled the trigger. Could it have been the Holy Spirit? Incidentally, I hid the pistol that day where Dad would never find it.

Two months after the shooting incident, Dad was still unemployed. His depression had worsened, he hadn't worked in months, and his drinking was increasing to a dangerous level. Then one day, the telephone rang. It was Dad's brother Merle calling from California. There was an employment opportunity at a bowling alley for a mechanic. Dad was on the next bus to California.

Several months passed before I finally got a short letter (one paragraph) from him. Then one day, without any notice, Dad walked through the front door. We greeted him with hugs and excitement! He stayed a few days and then returned to California.

Two or three weeks after Dad returned to California, we received a frightening telephone call. He had been in a life-threatening accident. As he was leaving work, out the side door, the unthinkable happened. As he approached the glass exit door, his heel caught in the cuff of his work pants, and he fell headfirst into the thick-plate glass door, crashing completely through it. Dad got up from the ground, went to his car, retrieved some clean rags, and held his face together until the ambulance arrived. He was sliced on both sides of his mouth down to his jawbone. His lower lip was hanging below his chinbone like a rubber flap, and the end of his nose was sliced off. The doctors estimated he lost over two pints of blood before suturing his face back together.

The accident happened at night, and his car was parked in the back of the bowling alley. If he would have been knocked unconscious at the point of impact into that plate glass door, Dad would have most likely bled to death. Some people may say, "Well, after all, he was a professional wrestler previously, and he knew how to take a hit. Maybe he was just hard to knock out." I believe differently. Grandma Elizabeth's prayers of protection were still following him. The Holy Spirit was there with him through that horrible accident, and once again, Dad's life was spared.

Two months had passed since Dad's accident when Mom suddenly informed us that we were moving to southern California. I couldn't believe what I was hearing and was hoping she wasn't serious. We had lived in Indianola, Iowa, for three years, and I had spent the first two years tolerating a few bullies. But during the third year, things had changed. I had been on the junior high school track team (seventh and eighth graders), and the coaches were aware of my speed. After the eighth-grade track season, I had gained respect from some of the varsity track team. Coach Starr had the sprinters run time trials in the 100-yard dash, and because I had the fastest time, I became the starting sprinter and earned the anchor position on the four-man 440-yard relay. At the beginning of the season, the older teammates did not like that and, at first, did not engage with me as a team member. After all, I was in the ninth grade, and my teammates were two to three years older. But after winning the first four track meets and being undefeated in the 440-yard relay, I was accepted, and I gained their friendship. Now finally, the bullies left me alone. Incidentally, Dad never saw any track meets and the success that my teammates and I had that season.

Now back to Mother's announcement that we were moving to California. When I finally realized that Mom was serious that we were leaving Indianola, a panic set in. I had new friends and got respect from students and teachers, and many of them had become my extended family. And now I was losing them. In desperation, I asked my Sunday school teacher, Bill Nyswonger, if I could live with him and his wife and finish high school in Indianola. Ultimately, Bill decided that he didn't think it would work. So on June 13, we left Indianola and headed west. Five days later, we met Dad and my uncle Merle and drove to our new residence in Van Nuys, California, about twenty miles northwest of downtown Los Angeles.

During the next seven years, my family experienced a lot of changes. Mom had a scare with ovarian cancer, but surgery saved her life. I graduated from Birmingham High School and attended college. My sisters had acquired jobs, and my sister Sandra married her high school sweetheart. My dad's drinking worsened, and at age forty-nine, he had a major stroke, which slowed him down physically. After his recovery from his stroke, he continued to drink heavily. Six months after his stroke, he had completely rehabilitated himself and was working full-time again as a mechanic.

One night, I received a telephone call from my mom, and she sounded distressed. After thirty years of marriage, Mom had finally had enough of my dad's drinking, and she told me she had filed for divorce. Dad then moved to South Central Los Angeles, a predominantly black community, where he quickly made new friends. I believe that was when God finally cornered him where he had nowhere else to run. He had very little money and a "road beater" car, and his health was failing. During the next three years, Dad encountered several more life-threatening situations. I will share several more of those potentially deadly experiences.

It was late one evening in 1970 when Dad pulled into the parking lot of a liquor store to stock up on more vodka. He parked near the front door where the driveway sloped toward a very busy boulevard. As he began to enter the store, something caught his attention. The vehicle parked next to his began to roll backward toward the street. There was an elderly lady sitting in the passenger seat. Dad quickly attempted to open the driver's door, but it was locked. He then ran behind the rolling vehicle and attempted to stop it, but there was a problem. An oil slick on the pavement caused him to slip, and he fell to the asphalt. He only had time to pull his upper body away from the rear wheels, and unfortunately, the car ran over both of his lower legs. By that time, several people got behind the moving car and stopped it from going into heavy traffic.

A few days after the accident, I went to visit him, and I could hardly believe my eyes. Both of his ankles and calf muscles were very swollen and looked like sofa pillows. You may not believe this, but miraculously, not a bone had been broken, no blood clots developed, and there was no major damage to his ankles. Dad was able to attend to his basic needs and return to normal activities in about three weeks. Once again, I guess luck was on his side, or was Grandma's intercessory prayers still preserving his life?

As I mentioned earlier, my dad was an extremely tough man and could endure severe pain. Several months after the parking lot accident, Dad was driving northbound on the San Diego Freeway when a speeding car sideswiped the left side of his car, sending him up the side of a fairly steep embankment. Dad's car was traveling about fifty-five miles per hour at the time of impact. The driver's door flew open, and Dad fell out of the car, landing on the ground, which was covered with ice plant—a low-growing succulent. Thankfully, this ground cover helped cushion his impact when he hit the ground. He told me that after sliding and bouncing on the ground, he just laid there, thinking maybe he was in shock. Slowly he began taking inventory of his body parts, and when Dad found nothing missing, he stood up and walked down the slope to a policeman who had just arrived. The police officer greeted Dad by saying, "Oh! I thought you were dead. I was going to check on you in a few minutes." Remarkably, Dad only had scratches and bruises on his body. He refused to go to the hospital to be examined. He was fifty-six years old when he hit the ground at high speed and only sustained scratches and bruises! I guess once again, Dad was lucky, or was God still honoring Grandma's prayers?

A few months after the car accident on the San Diego Freeway, Dad decided to go to a carryout restaurant called Chicken Delight. The restaurant was not far from where he lived in South Central Los

Angeles. It was at night, and as Dad was walking back to his car with his chicken dinner, four young black men approached him and began to taunt him. They encircled Dad and began pushing him around. Suddenly, one of the men hit him over the head with a glass bottle. The bottle broke, and Dad fell to the asphalt on the broken glass. In those days, it was in style to wear shoes that had thick wooden heels. As Dad lay on the asphalt, the men stomped on his hands as he attempted to get up, driving the shards of glass into his fingers and palms. They then stomped on his head with their shoes with wooden heels creating large indentations on his bald head.

Dad survived that terrible beating, not because he was tough and strong but because God's hand of mercy was extended over him, and his life was spared. God continued to honor the intercessory prayers of Elizabeth Pease even though she had died twenty-five years earlier.

I visited Dad after that vicious attack, and once again, I was amazed how quickly he had recovered. I felt the indentations on his bald head and saw his scarred hands where the glass had penetrated. As he shared with me what had happened that night, he seemed bewildered and deeply troubled. Dad did not understand why those young men attacked and nearly beat him to death. He neither showed any bitterness nor did he speak derogatory words toward those young men. If only those men could have known that Dad loved black people and that he would have defended and fought to protect them if they had been the ones being attacked. Unlike my dad, I struggled to forgive those men who nearly took his life in such a brutal way. In time, I was able to pray for and forgive those young men and be free from the anger that was inside me. The head injuries sustained in that beating precipitated another major stroke several months later that ended his life.

Oh, I almost forgot to mention something that is important. I stated earlier that my dad was a paint contractor, and there were several times that Dad was on a ladder or scaffold when he fell several feet to the ground. He would simply get up, brush himself off, climb back up to the scaffold, and continue painting. He never broke a bone or suffered any injures in those falls. Once again, I guess he was just lucky, or was there someone softening his falls when he hit the ground?

By now, you should see a pattern of God's intervention that continuously spared my father's life over and over throughout the years. Dad's survival was beyond luck; it was the result of God honoring Grandma Elizabeth's intercessory prayers that kept him alive until his eyes could be opened to the Word of God and accept Jesus as Lord and Savior. No matter what the devil threw at my dad—rejection, physical and emotional pain, horrific accidents, and dad's own destructive behavior—the devil could not destroy him. Why? Because God answered the effectual, fervent prayers of an intercessor. Intercessory prayer built a hedge of protection that encompassed my dad's life so he would not be destroyed until he would have an encounter with Jesus Christ. Oh! What a Savior!

In the next section of this book, I will share the wonderful experience of my dad's new spiritual birth into God's kingdom through Jesus Christ. To be born again is to be brought forth as a child into God's kingdom through our Savior. When we are in Christ, we become a new creature, all the "old things are passed away; behold, all things are become new" (II Corinthians 5:17).

Redemption

During 1970, I became involved with a ministry called Action Life. On Friday and Saturday nights, we would pair up and go to city parks and shopping malls and share Jesus with people who would stop and listen. God blessed our outreach efforts, and many people prayed with us to receive Jesus Christ as Lord and Savior. After strangers prayed to receive Jesus as Savior, we would get their names and telephone numbers and would follow up to anchor them in the Word of God with literature and fellowship. Also, we would always invite them to meet us at a friend's home on Wednesday nights to sing, have Bible study, and be part of the Action Life group.

One night, in November 1971, we returned to Dave's house after sharing Jesus in the Fallbrook Mall. We were singing and worshipping, and at the end of the praise time, two young men sat beside me and asked, "Gary, what's wrong?" Apparently, I looked distressed during the time of worship. These two young men had been saved through our street ministry a few months earlier. I told them that I had been praying for my dad's salvation since I was a child, and over the last two years, he was becoming belligerent, losing his memory, and drinking nearly every day until he would pass out. I feared he would die soon. I told the young converts that most of my life, I struggled with the thought that he wouldn't make heaven. Then one of the young men asked, "How have you been praying for him?"

I asked, "What do you mean how have I been praying for him?" I suddenly felt defensive. After all, I had been saved since I was six years old, and I had been preaching for about three years. How could they ask me how had I been praying for my father's salvation?

The young man again asked, "No, really, how have you been praying for your dad all these years?"

I stated that I prayed by saying, "Lord, save my dad and don't let him go to hell."

One of the men blurted out, "That's not enough!"

Suddenly, I felt myself become a little angry. I started to argue with them when I heard a still small voice say, "Be silent. This is what I have wanted you to know all of your life." I obeyed that still small voice and listened to their instruction that became a revelation to me on how to pray for the unsaved. The young convert declared, "What your dad needs is deliverance from addiction to alcohol. He has been blinded by the devil, and he cannot hear the voice of the Lord because of his depression and alcoholism." Then we all prayed together, and their authoritative prayer went as follows: In prayer, they specifically mentioned my dad by name to the Lord. They took authority over Satan's grip on my dad's life, and in the name of Jesus Christ, they commanded the devil to set him free and to take the blinders off his eyes so Dad could finally hear the gospel and respond and receive Jesus as Savior. Then one of the young men prayed, "Father, send a messenger to Eddie Hopkins while he is free from Satan's control and while his eyes and ears are open to the gospel." Then together all three of us claimed my dad to the kingdom of God and, by faith, proclaimed salvation over his life in the name of Jesus Christ. I did not know, at that time, that I would be the messenger who would deliver the gospel of love to my dad a few weeks later.

After that prayer time with those young men, my faith soared within me for the salvation of my dad as never before. I must caution you that my prayer of faith concerning my dad's deliverance and salvation would be sorely tested. More on that later.

Before I continue, I want to ask you to do something. The above teaching, and there is more on how to pray for the unsaved, may be new or foreign to you. I pray that you will keep your mind and heart open and receive these words into your spirit. This teaching may be what the Lord has wanted you to know all your life. The Bible tells us that when Mary, the mother of Jesus, heard a word from the Lord, she pondered it in her heart. In other words, Mary kept it in her memory and meditated on it.

A few weeks had passed since those two young men prayed for my father's salvation, and it was getting close to Christmas. I was trying to decide what to buy for my dad. He did not need T-shirts, socks, or a necktie, so I asked the Lord to help me find something that would provide some spiritual blessing or insight for him. I went to the Bible bookstore in Van Nuys and was searching through different material when I saw a paperback book titled *Good News for Modern Man*. I read several pages and realized I had found the perfect gift for him. It is written in today's English version. It's like reading the daily newspaper. Fortunately, even though Dad only had a ninth-grade education, he was a good reader. Every Saturday morning, when he was home, he would sit at the kitchen table and read *Field & Stream* magazine because he enjoyed reading about hunting and fishing.

Okay, I bought the *Good News for Modern Man* book, and I was filled with anticipation; I could hardly wait to give it to Dad. My wife and I drove to South Central Los Angeles on Christmas Eve, December 1971. I was filled with excitement as we pulled into his driveway. I was expecting to see a big change in my father. After all, we had prayed for his deliverance and salvation just a few weeks earlier. Well, so much for expectations. I had to repeatedly ring the doorbell and knock on the front door for two or three minutes. Finally, he opened the door and just stood there, staring at us for several seconds. At first, I didn't think he was going to invite us into his house. When we entered, he didn't say hi or offer a hug; he just lit a cigarette, sat down on the sofa, and stared at the floor. This was a familiar scene I had witnessed for several years whenever I would visit. Nothing had changed since our prayer of faith concerning Dad's redemption. I felt my heart sink, and I was almost overwhelmed with disappointment. I tried not to show my feelings of sadness in front of Dad. I did my best to stay cheerful. That wasn't easy, especially when he was so depressed. He said there was nothing to live for and that he would be better off dead. I had heard these same words from him years earlier when we lived in Iowa.

Dad was in bad shape mentally. He was losing his memory and had trouble engaging with us. I tried to be positive and said, "Dad, I brought you a Christmas gift. I didn't buy you socks or T-shirts because I knew you didn't need them."

He asked, "Well, what is it?" After handing it to him, he slowly unwrapped the gift; and when he saw it was a book, he asked what was it about. I told him that it was the New Testament written in plain English and was written like the daily newspaper. That's why it's titled *Good News for Modern Man*. I then said, in a joking way, "I paid five dollars for the book, and if you don't want it, I'll take it back." He had no comment. I then asked him if he would really read it.

He mumbled, in a low voice, "Yeah."

I asked him, "Dad, do you promise?"

He slowly looked up at me, and after a thoughtful pause, he said, "I promise." This was the *second promise* he ever made to me. My memory quickly went back years ago when I walked into our garage when he was about to hang himself. Remember in part 1 of this story, I went to the garage to feed my pet hawk; and when I entered the garage, Dad was sitting on the stepladder with a noose hanging above him, about to end his life. At that time, I asked him if he would come into the house and watch wrestling on the television with me instead of ending his life. When he said yes, I then asked him if he promised, and he answered, "I promise." Do you recall that I stated that was the first time Dad had ever made a promise to me? Now twelve years later, on Christmas Eve, he made a second promise to me that he would read the book. That second promise to read the book would become the most important promise he ever kept!

We left Dad's home and drove back to San Bernardino where we lived. While driving discouragement flooded my mind, and I needed a word from the Lord. I recalled Hebrews 11:1 (ESV), which says, "Now faith is the assurance of things hoped for, the conviction of things not seen." The KJV states, "Now faith is the substance of things hoped for, the evidence of things not seen." Hebrews 11:1 replaced my discouragement with hope and joy. The words *of things hoped for* speaks of future hope in answered prayer. Just because I didn't see a spiritual change in my dad on Christmas Eve didn't mean that the prayer for Dad's redemption wasn't going to take place in the future. Secondly, the words *of things not seen* tells me there is a reality that I couldn't see on that Christmas Eve. The reality that I couldn't see is that heaven was moving in behalf of our prayer of deliverance and redemption concerning my dad, and in God's timing, we would see the fruition of our prayer of salvation come to pass.

As believers, we must be led not by what we see but by the Word of God concerning faith, hope, healing, deliverance, and the salvation of our loved ones. St. Paul tells us, "While we look not at the things which are seen, for the things which are seen are temporal, but the things which are not seen are eternal" (2 Corinthians 4:18). Other believers may see it differently, but that is the inspiration and encouragement I received from Hebrews 11:1 and Second Corinthians. At that moment, I decided, by faith, I would see my dad delivered and saved and would never again entertain the thought that he may spend eternity in hell. You may not agree with the above words, but please stay with me. In part 2 of this book, I will provide scriptures that support the above teaching, especially on how to pray for the unsaved and see them saved.

When we arrived home on Christmas Eve, I asked the Lord how could Dad's physical condition worsen and why he became more despondent after we prayed for his deliverance. In time, the Lord showed me the answer. There was spiritual warfare taking place between heaven and hell, and the devil was in a battle to keep Dad's soul. The devil was doing everything he could to keep his grip on my dad.

I prayed and asked the Lord for understanding, and I turned to Daniel 10:12–13 for the answer. Prophet Daniel had had a vision concerning his people and Israel, and Daniel prayed for understanding of that vision. Twenty days had past, but Daniel had not received an answer. But then something miraculous happened. In verse 10, an angel appeared to Daniel with the answer to his prayer. The angel explained to Daniel why it took twenty-one days to deliver the answer, and in that explanation, we get a little glimpse of the battle that rages between God's heavenly beings (angels) and hell's demons.

In verse 12 to 14, the angel explained to Daniel that he encountered satanic opposition in his attempt to bring the answer to Daniel. Daniel 10:12 (KJV) reads as follows: "Then said he unto me, 'Fear not Daniel: for from the first day that thou didst set thine heart to understand, and to chasten thyself before thy God, thy words were heard, and I am come for thy words.'"

The angel continued in verses 13, 14: "But the prince of the kingdom of Persia withstood me one and twenty days: but, lo, Michael, one of the chief princes, came to help me; and I remained there with the kings of Persia. Now I am come to make you understand…" It's important to note that the prince of Persia was one of the demons who worked to oppose God's people. The Lord then brought to my memory Ephesians 6:12 (KJV), "For we wrestle not against flesh and blood, but against principalities, against powers, against the rulers of the darkness of this world, against spiritual wickedness in high places." The above scriptures gave me comfort and reassured me that my heavenly Father had heard our prayers from the night we first prayed for Dad's deliverance and salvation and that the spiritual battle was on for Dad's soul. Satan and his demons tremble at the name of Jesus; they get nervous and must flee from Christ's presence. I then knew that heaven was moving on behalf of my dad and that God agreed with our prayer of faith concerning my dad's soul and that we, in time, would see the results of our prayers.

I realized that God is working out all things according to his own will. That is probably one of the main reasons for delayed answers to our prayers, but when a loved one is sick and dying, he or she may not have years remaining to hear and respond to the gospel. Such was the situation with my dad. He didn't have years remaining to hear and respond to the voice of the Lord. He had only months to live, and we needed a miracle.

Two months had passed since I gave the book to Dad for Christmas, and we decided to visit him one afternoon. As we drove into his driveway, I was prepared once again to bang on the front door until he woke up from a deep sleep. But this time, I didn't have to bang on the door until my knuckles were sore. To my surprise, within seconds after I first knocked on the door, it opened, and there stood a sober man with a big smile on his face! He looked ten years younger and greeted us by saying, "Kids, come in. I have something wonderful to tell you!" He gave me a long embrace, and then for the first time in my life, he said, "Gary, I love you." As you can imagine, I was in shock; I couldn't even speak! Dad then said, "Please sit down. I have something to share with you." He began to tell us the events that happened after that Christmas Eve. The following is his testimony:

"After you left on Christmas Eve, I continued to drink and stayed drunk for two days or so. Finally, I woke up and realized I needed to eat. I fixed a sandwich and set on the sofa to watch television. I then noticed the book *Good News for Modern Man* sitting on the coffee table. After I finished my sandwich, I decided I didn't want the book in the house, so I took it to the garage and placed it on a shelf by a small window. I returned to the house and began drinking again until I passed out. Two or three weeks passed, and I decided I couldn't live like this anymore. It was time to 'check out.' After placing personal items in a large container—things I thought you would want, Gary—I headed for the garage. I got the stepladder, placed it under a beam, and secured the cord to the beam. I didn't want the cord to fail. Then I made a noose at the end of the cord and was about to put it over my head when I noticed a book on the shelf by the little window. It was the *Good News for Modern Man*. The sun was shining through the window, and the book looked as though it was glowing. Then I remembered I had promised you that I would read it. I told myself that I could die another day. I went into the house, made some coffee, sat down, and began to read. I started with the book of Matthew, then Mark, Luke, and John. After I finished those four books, I read them again. As I finished the book of John the second time, I suddenly felt a presence of something in my living room that I had never felt or known before. It wasn't scary; it was beautiful. I was feeling a presence of love and joy that is hard to explain. Then I felt my strength leave my body, and I fell forward to the floor on my hands and knees. And I cried out, 'Jesus, you are my Lord. I accept you as my Savior.' I felt clean. I felt all the anger and bitterness leave me, and I experienced the feeling of love for the first time. I forgave my mother for her cruelty and wanted her to know that I loved her."

Dad continued to say that he had a compelling desire to share with people his experience with Jesus Christ. The only church he knew was in Van Nuys, where I attended as a teenager. He said on a Sunday morning, he walked into that church; and just before the preaching started, he stood up and shared with the people in that congregation how the presence of the Holy Spirit came and filled his living room with peace and love. Dad told them God had delivered him from bondage, and he confessed Jesus Christ as Lord and Savior.

Just think, when the Holy Spirit filled Dad's living room and when he fell to his knees, there was no one singing gospel music. There wasn't a preacher giving an altar call. It was the presence of the Holy Spirit and the Word of God that Dad responded to. Where the Spirit of the Lord is, there is liberty.

At the end of my visit with Dad that day, he showed me the book *Good News for Modern Man*. He had read it so much the pages were nearly falling out. Dad asked me to get him another copy, which I did promptly. A picture of the second copy that I gave him is in the last pages of this book.

In Romans 10:9–10, Paul tells us how a person becomes saved or born again. Paul declares, "That if thou shalt confess with thy mouth the Lord Jesus, and shalt believe in thine heart that God hath raised him from the dead, thou shalt be saved. For with the heart man believeth unto righteousness and with the mouth confession is made unto salvation." This is what my dad did in his home and on that Sunday morning in church. How I wish I could have been at that church service to see my dad stand up in front of people and give his testimony! Dad had never spoken in front of a group of people in his life, and he would have rather taken a physical beating than talk in front of a congregation. Before he was saved, he couldn't even lead in silent prayer. Now he could stand up and share his testimony before a large group of people where before, Dad only had confidence in his element, which was in the wrestling ring or fighting in bars. For him to stand before people and share his salvation experience was a miracle in and of itself. But you see, Dad had become a new creature in Christ. Second Corinthians 5:17 tells us, "Therefore, if any man be in Christ, he is a new creature, old things are passed away, behold, all things are become new."

The reason Dad felt peace during and after his salvation experience was that he was now in harmony with the Creator and all of heaven. He was no longer a stranger or foreigner to God and heaven, but he had been made a member of the family of God. He was now accepted into the beloved when he received Jesus Christ as Savior and confessed Christ as Lord (Romans 10:9–10).

It's important to mention that Dad always believed in the existence of God and his Son, Jesus. When my sisters and I were young, he would not let Mom tell us there was a Santa Claus. Dad insisted that we knew Christmas was about the birth of Jesus Christ. Sadly, Dad didn't think that Jesus could or would ever accept him because he didn't believe he was good enough or worthy to be loved by God. Dad did not experience love as a child; instead, he was abused and neglected by his parents. This made it extremely difficult for him to believe he was loved and accepted by a God he could not see or touch. As a child, Dad only saw a punishing God that demanded goodness and perfection. Even though Grandma Elizabeth knew how to intercede in prayer for Dad's physical protection, he still grew up in a harsh and strict environment put forth by the women in the household. Also, Dad's father and grandfather were neither good role models nor were they good providers.

What a shame the gospel of love and grace was not shown in Dad's home. The gospel of grace tells us that God so loved us that he sent his only begotten Son to earth to be born of a virgin. He lived a sinless life, died on a cruel cross, shed his incorruptible blood, descended into the lower parts of the earth, and rose again from the dead so that by believing in and having faith in Jesus Christ, our sins are washed away, and we receive eternal life!

From this point forward to the end of part 1, I want to reach out to you readers who do not know Jesus Christ as your personal Savior. You may not be controlled or blinded by addiction to drugs or alcohol, but maybe you have been abused mentally and physically by someone who should have loved you. Maybe you have been betrayed and are in a prison of heartache or are bound by unforgiveness and anger toward God. Some of you reading this may not even care about God or may deny God's existence. To you who don't believe in God, you are in bondage by your own unbelief. St. Paul tells us in 2 Corinthians 4:4, "In whom the god of this world [the devil] hath blinded the minds of them which believe not, lest the light of the glorious Gospel of Christ, who is the image of God, should shine unto them." Many of us have been blinded by unbelief, sorrow, anger, or unforgiveness. No matter where you are spiritually or emotionally, I have good news! Jesus came to this world not to condemn it but to save the people who are in it—you and me.

Jesus told us what his mission and calling was in the book of Luke 4:18 when he said, "The Spirit of the Lord is upon me because He hath anointed me to preach the Gospel to the poor; He hath sent me to heal the broken-hearted, to preach deliverance to the captives, restore sight to the blind, to set at liberty them that are bruised, to preach the acceptable year of the Lord."

Jesus Christ did all the above for Dad! Jesus brought the gospel to my dad when he read the book *Good News for Modern Man*. My dad was delivered from the grip of addiction. He was spiritually blind, but Jesus opened his eyes so he could see the light of the gospel and respond to it. Jesus liberated my dad from the bruising that Satan had inflicted on him all his life.

You may have believed a lie that you aren't good enough or worthy to be loved by Jesus Christ, just like my dad once believed. The biggest lie ever perpetrated by the devil is that "You have served yourself and the flesh and me all your life, and now you want to receive Jesus Christ as Savior? Who do you think you are? How dare you try to do that now? God won't accept you." Satan is a liar! We cannot receive salvation and eternal life by being good and doing good deeds. Salvation through Jesus Christ is a gift. You cannot earn it by good works, lest any man boasts. You receive forgiveness, cleansing, salvation by faith and by putting your trust in Jesus Christ. You don't earn salvation by your performance of good works. Your salvation is secured by Christ's performance, by what he did on the cross.

My dad's anger, low self-esteem, and guilt created a wall or veil between himself and Jesus Christ. His self-loathing became a barrier that hindered him from coming to Jesus Christ for salvation. In the Old Testament, there was a veil in the temple that separated the Jewish people from the holy of holies, the mercy seat of God. Only the priest could go behind that veil and offer God a blood sacrifice for the forgiveness of the sins of the people. But when Jesus shed his incorruptible blood on the cross and sacrificed his life for us, the veil that was separating people from God was ripped from the top to the bottom when Christ cried out from the cross, "It is finished!" Now anyone can come freely and openly to Christ for deliverance, salvation, and healing.

Friends, has your past crippled you? Do you feel broken? Jesus has never met a broken heart or bruised life that he cannot heal. He has never found a hopeless case spiritually, and there is no sin so great that God cannot forgive. When a person looks to Jesus and receives him as Savior, their past and sins are removed from them as far as the east is from the west (Psalm 103:12). This sounds like a paradox, but the scripture is telling us that when we are born again, our old life is forever moving away from us, never to be seen again by the Lord. The book of Isaiah 38:17 tells us that God has cast all our sins behind his back. The book of Micah 7:19 says that God will cast all our sins into the depths of the sea, never to be remembered anymore. These scriptures are telling us that when we come to Jesus and become born again, the old life, as an unbeliever, is gone. It is as though that old life never existed. Jesus can save you to the uttermost!

The blood that flowed through Christ's veins still breaks addiction's chains, and it still heals and restores every person who believes in him and confesses Jesus as their personal Savior. Are you ready to leave sorrow, addictions, and guilt behind you and know Jesus as your personal Savior? Do you want to be free from the thing or things that have taken you captive and to have your past washed away and to receive eternal life through Jesus Christ? Then pray this simple prayer:

"Heavenly Father, I come to you in the name of Jesus Christ. I believe that Jesus is the Son of God, who shed his blood on a cross and died for me. The third day, he rose from the dead and ascended into heaven and now sits at the right hand of the heavenly Father. Lord, I believe you have heard my prayer and that my sins are gone! For by faith, I accept Jesus as my Lord and Savior, and I thank you that I have eternal life through faith in Jesus Christ."

If you prayed that prayer, you have become a new creature in Christ. You now belong to a new family—the family of God here on earth and in heaven. It is now important for you to find a group of believers or a church where you can tell other Christians that you have accepted Jesus as your Savior. It is important to be around other believers for fellowship and to learn more about the love of God and his will for your life. If you were sincere when you prayed that prayer to receive Jesus as your Savior, I will meet you someday. Maybe not here on earth, but one day, I'll meet and greet you in heaven.

I highly suggest that you contact a local church in your area where you can worship and have fellowship with Christian believers. If you do, talk to the pastor and tell him about your decision to receive Christ as your savior. He will be thrilled to meet you and hear your testimony. Welcome to God's family.

Part Two

Praying for the Unsaved

Through the years, people have asked me how to know if it is God's will for a person to be saved and have eternal life. This is a question that every Christian should be asking. Most Christians believe there is an eternal hell and a lake of fire that burns forever. This is not the place for me to discuss the theology of hell, whether hell is temporal or forever. I want to merely point out that the very thought of someone you love, especially a family member, may go to hell is horrifying and can torture a person mentally. Whether hell lasts one day or forever, both are too long. I lived with that fear, concerning where my dad would spend eternity, until I was twenty-six years old.

When I was ten years old, I wanted my dad to be saved so badly I played gospel music over and over when he would take afternoon naps on the sofa. I was hoping the words in the songs about salvation would penetrate his heart and mind, and he would accept Jesus as Savior.

I wrote in part 1 that my mother was a born-again Christian, and to her credit, she never spoke badly about my dad. Even though he was not a good provider and was absent from us most of the time, Mom did not speak evil words about him; she always instructed us to love and pray for our dad. She taught us a simple prayer that went like this: "Lord, please save our dad and don't let him go to hell."

I wrote in part 1 that that kind of prayer was insufficient to get my dad delivered and saved. He needed deliverance from the addiction to alcohol that had controlled him since he was sixteen years old. His addiction to alcohol increased his depression, lowered his self-worth, and increased his self-loathing. Dad was trapped; he had been snared by the fowler (the devil) and did not know how to escape. The Word tells us in Psalm 91:3, "Surely, he shall deliver thee from the snare of the fowler, and from the destructive pestilence." A fowler is a bird catcher that sets up a net or a trap to catch birds, and when caught in the snare, a bird cannot get free by itself. But because of Jesus Christ, we who have been born again have escaped the snare of the fowler. The net has been torn, and we have slipped away from the snare into the arms of Jesus. When a person is snared by the devil, it is impossible to escape by their own efforts; they need a savior. That is why believers must intercede in prayer for those who are snared. My dad was in a spiritual wilderness snared by the devil for many years, and he needed to be freed by a deliverer.

Many have been snared or held captive by something. It may have been by unbelief, lies about God, being a part of a cult, or because of addictions. I believe that if you are born again (saved), it is because someone prayed for you, and a messenger brought the Word of God into your life. The message of salvation may have been brought into your life through gospel music, preaching, or reading the Word of God.

As believers, this is our high calling that we would be witnesses to the world, telling the lost about his grace and mercy. People need to know that God, through Jesus Christ, has reconciled the world unto himself, and we have been given the ministry of reconciliation (2 Corinthians 5:18–19). In other words, when Jesus Christ shed his incorruptible blood on the cross, he made atonement for our sins. *Atonement* means "making amends or reparation for our sin." We need to tell people everywhere, when we have the opportunity, that Christ came to rescue them spiritually and not to condemn them. Second Corinthians 5:21 tells us, "For he [God] hath made him to be sin for us, who knew no sin; that we might be made the righteousness of God in Him." Tell the unsaved if they accept Jesus as Savior and put their faith in Christ (Yeshua), they become a new creature in Christ and receive eternal life through faith in him (2 Corinthians 5:17).

When Jesus died on the cross, he took on our filthiness, wickedness, and all our sin (2 Corinthians 5:21). When we believe in him for our salvation, we get his righteousness, goodness, and wisdom and become partakers of his inheritance in heaven. *What an exchange!* This is the good news of the gospel.

I realize, as believers, you know this already, but I believe we all need to hear the good news again and again, lest we take for granted what Jesus Christ did for us at Calvary. Please do not make it difficult for people to come to Christ by presenting religious dogma and legalistic dos and don'ts or by telling them they must change their lifestyle in order to be saved. Tell them of the love of God and share the scriptures I have mentioned in this book. Let the Holy Spirit finish the Lord's work in their lives. As ambassadors of Christ, we are to be witnesses and messengers of the good news.

Unworthiness

Unfortunately, Dad incorrectly thought he had to "clean up" his life morally before he could come to Jesus for salvation. He was consumed with guilt and shame because he didn't believe he deserved or was worthy to be loved by God.

Several years ago, I had a friend who was dying of lung cancer. Bob was a kind and friendly person, always available when someone needed a helping hand. When Bob was close to death, I asked his wife, Sue, if he would be open to discuss salvation and eternal life. This was Bob's response: "I have served the world and ignored Jesus all my life, and now that I am dying, I'm not going to ask Jesus to save me." Bob thought running to Jesus would be cowardly and that he didn't deserve heaven. How incredibly sad. Bob believed in God, but like my father, he didn't believe he was worthy of heaven. Friends, nobody is worthy of salvation and heaven; it is a gift from God. We receive eternal life by faith through the grace of Jesus Christ.

Unworthiness is a weapon of the devil. It is a lie put forth by Satan to keep people from coming to the feet of Jesus. Believing you are not worthy to come to Jesus is a denial of Christ's righteousness that has been granted to you when he shed his incorruptible blood for you at Calvary. If a person is waiting until he is perfect before coming to Christ for salvation, he will never be saved. No one can impress God by coming to him, bragging about all their good works. God's righteousness is received by faith unto all who believe (Romans 3:21–26). A person's good works are not the measuring stick of righteousness. Jesus Christ is our righteousness, and we take on his righteousness when we receive him and confess him as Savior by faith.

The negative thoughts Dad had about himself and God became a wall or a curtain that hindered his entrance to the holy of holies, where he could find salvation and have fellowship with Jesus Christ. Dad was wrong. I wrote in part 1 that the veil in the temple was ripped from the top to the bottom when Jesus cried out from the cross, "It is finished." There are no longer conditions, physical barriers, or religious rituals that must be performed before coming to the mercy seat of God. The veils of guilt, shame, and unworthiness that have kept people from coming to Jesus have been removed. The wall of unworthiness that once stood between my Dad and God has been torn down. Your loved ones can come openly and freely to Jesus just as they are for healing and salvation. What a *wonderful Savior* we have!

Now all mankind can come boldly to the throne of grace to receive mercy and salvation and to have fellowship with the Lord in time of need (Hebrews 4:16). *Boldly* means "we can come to the heavenly Father, in the name of Jesus, with freedom to speak what is hurting us and have confidence that he will accept and hear us." Jesus said, "Come unto me all you that labor and are heavy laden and I will give you rest" (Mathew 11:28). Christ was speaking to those who are weighed down with sin and those laden with the cares of this world. Go to him, and he will give you rest—rest from the burden of sin by cleansing you and giving you eternal life and rest from worry and discouragement. "Casting all your cares upon him, because he careth for you" (1 Peter 5:7). What greater need can a person have other than the need for salvation?

I said the above to remind you that we serve a chain-breaking God. The blood of Jesus can break the grip of addictions and any besetting or controlling habit that is preventing your loved ones from coming to him. What is the most important thing God wants or desires? God wants us to be in good health and to prosper as our soul prospers, of course. Ponder this fact: that every person who was healed by Jesus, no matter how great the miracle, eventually died. Every person who accepts Christ as their Savior lives for eternity and never dies. God gave up his only Son so that mankind could be redeemed (John 3:16). God reconciled the world through the death and resurrection of Jesus Christ and thereby reclaimed the world and mankind back to himself. John the Baptist declared, "Behold the lamb of God that takes away the sin of the world." At Calvary, God's creation manhandled the creator (Jesus). God allowed it to happen so he could rescue and redeem you and me.

I believe it is obvious that God's priority is to see people born again by accepting his Son as their personal Savior. God gave up his only Son so he could get to you and me. What a loving heavenly Father he is.

When your position of faith comes under attack, hold up the shield of faith. That is your greatest weapon of spiritual warfare, and it defeats the enemy's darts when we use it. The shield of faith will quench every fiery dart of doubt, accusation, and fear that the enemy throws at you. Ephesians 6:13 says, "And having done all, to stand, stand therefore…" St. Paul in Ephesians says, "Put on the whole armor of God." The Lord did not leave us defenseless, without protection from the wiles of the devil. When the attacks come—and they will—plant that shield faith in front of you, refuse to back down, refuse to be moved, like a good soldier in battle, and hold on to your declaration of faith with all perseverance.

When we put on the whole armor of God, only one part of our body is vulnerable and exposed—our backside! So never turn and run during the battle. It is encouraging to know that as long as we hold our position of faith, God has promised to be our rear reward, which means he will be our rear guard. He has us covered, and no spiritual enemy can sneak up behind and defeat us.

Webster's Dictionary says the word *quench* means "to extinguish a fire, to put out the glowing coals [fiery darts] with water or oil." I believe the oil and water are symbols of the Holy Spirit and the Word of God. The God kind of faith contains the oil, the anointing of the Holy Spirit, and the water is the Word of God. Both the oil and the washing of the water of the Word quench all fiery darts. For the yoke of bondage shall be destroyed because of the anointing (Isaiah 10:27).

In Romans 10:17, we are told that "Faith comes by hearing and hearing the word of God." Hearing what the Word of God has to say about effective prayer, especially when praying for the unsaved, will increase your faith when you pray for their salvation. My desire is to increase your faith when you pray for the deliverance and salvation of your loved ones by exercising effective and accurate prayer—one that brings results. In 1 Timothy 4:6, St. Paul said, "That we are to be nourished up in the words of faith and of good doctrine." It is my prayer that the teaching in this book will do exactly that. May your faith be nourished and built up through the scriptures and this teaching.

The following pages will provide a host of scriptures that will show how to exercise your faith when you pray, especially for the unsaved.

God has chosen to use the prayers of the saints to bring his will to fruition on earth. We are instructed in 1 Timothy 2:1–2 (KJV), "Therefore, that, first of all, supplications, prayers, intercessions, and giving of thanks, be made for all men; for kings and for all that are in authority; that we may lead a quiet and peaceable life in all godliness and honesty." This type of prayer and intercession brings about the salvation of men and women.

God doesn't tell us to just sit back and he will take care of all the problems with rulers and society. He tells us to change situations in our community and in government with effectual prayer and inter-cessions so that we may live a quiet and peaceable life in all godliness. When we live a peaceable life, it is easier to spread the good news of the gospel of grace to our community and the nation. First Timothy 2:8 states, "I will therefore that men pray everywhere, lifting up holy hands, without wrath and doubting." Effective prayer and interces-sions change people's hearts and lives and our communities.

Hebrews 11:6 reads, "But without faith it is impossible to please him; for he that cometh to God must believe that he is, and that he is a rewarder of them that diligently seek him." When Eddie Hopkins was reading the four gospels of Matthew, Mark, Luke, and John, the word of God was being implanted and infused into his heart and mind. As he was reading the gospels for the second time, his faith was exponentially increasing. While Dad was reading the book of John for the second time, his heart was suddenly opened to receive Jesus

PART TWO
PRAYING FOR THE UNSAVED

as Savior. God's timing is perfect. When God saw that the door to Dad's heart was open, God sent the Holy Spirit rushing into Dad's living room. This caused Dad to fall to his hands and knees and cry out, "Jesus, you are my Savior, and I accept you as Lord."

Another example of God's perfect timing can be found in Acts 9:10–17. Ananias was a disciple of Jesus at Damascus, and he received a vision. In that vision, the Lord told him to go to the house of Judas and pray for a man named Saul (later renamed Paul). Saul had persecuted Christians and had perpetrated evil against the saints at Jerusalem for many years. Saul was on his way to Damascus to arrest any Christian he could find and bring them back to Jerusalem for punishment. I'm sure you know the story how Jesus showed up as a bright light from heaven, and Saul became blind and fell to the ground. Then the men who were with Saul took him to Damascus, to the house of Judas, where Ananias came and prayed for Saul three days later. Ananias laid hands on Saul, and Saul received his sight. Saul arose and was baptized, and Saul's ministry was launched. Think of God's timing. Jesus waited until Saul was on his way to Damascus so Saul could meet Ananias and be healed, saved, and baptized. Ananias was the messenger who brought the good news of grace to Paul.

Yes, Ananias was the messenger who led Saul (later named Paul) to a born-again experience, but there was another messenger who sewed the Word of God into Saul's life. That messenger was Stephen. In Acts 7, Stephen had been falsely accused of blasphemous words against Moses, God, and the law and was brought before the high priest and the council for trial. The priest asked Stephen if those accusations were true. The high priest allowed Stephen to speak in his defense for several minutes. Interestingly, Stephen never denied the charges but, instead, gave a history lesson to the Jews beginning with Abraham through the time of Jesus. Some commentators call Stephen's speech a lecture, but I believe Stephen delivered one of the greatest sermons ever recorded in the New Testament. Yes, he did discuss the rebelliousness of the Jewish people and that they had killed prophets, and Stephen referred to them as betrayers and murderers. These words may seem a little harsh, but Stephen preached to them

43

in love. We know that there was no malice in Stephen's heart because just before he was stoned, he prayed this prayer: "Lord, lay not this sin to their charge."

Saul not only consented to Stephen's execution but was also present when Stephen preached before his stoning (Acts 7:58). Just before the stones pummeled Stephen's body, he proclaimed Jesus as the Son of God to the angry crowd. Stephen said, "Behold, I see the heavens opened, and the Son of Man standing on the right hand of God." Stephen was possibly the first messenger to bring the gospel to Saul. While Saul stood, waiting to see Stephen killed, he heard the Word of God preached, and those words were infused into Saul's carnal mind. I believe those words of truth began to take root within Saul and that they began to soften his cold, hard heart.

It is paramount that we, in some manner, get the Word of God into people's hearts and lives. The message of God's love and saving grace can be given through songs, testimonies, the written word, and most importantly, by the demonstration of love to the lost. When Saul heard the Word of God, it prepared him for his encounter with Jesus on the road to Damascus. This is what my father, Eddie, experienced when he read the four gospels. The living word was being planted into fertile ground. When the scriptures took root in Dad's spirit, he cried out, "Jesus, My Lord and Savior."

We are not all called to be preachers, but we are all called to be witnesses (Isaiah 43:10, Acts 1:8). There must be a messenger to bring the gospel of saving grace to an unsaved individual. It may be a simple act of kindness, may be loving words of support, or may be making a statement such as, "Do you know your sins have been forgiven?" That should get their attention and spark a conversation.

As we know, it takes faith to believe in God and receive salvation through Jesus Christ. But did you know God has given a measure of faith to everyone? God has given everyone enough faith so when they hear the message of salvation, they can believe and receive Jesus as their Savior. What a great God! He has given us what we need, a measure of faith, so when we hear the gospel, we can believe (Romans 12:3).

When we are in a crisis or facing a mountain that looks nearly impossible to climb, we can't see what God is doing for us on the other side of that mountain. God is preparing a blessing, an answer to your prayers. Don't give up. It's coming. It's on the way. God is sending the answer to your petitions. That is what God did for Abraham and Isaac. God was testing Abraham's faith when he told Abraham to take his son Isaac to the mountain and sacrifice him on an altar of fire. While Abraham and Isaac were climbing up one side of the mountain, God was sending a ram up from the other side. Think of the mental torment Abraham suffered as he journeyed with his son up the mountain to slay him on an altar. I am sure Abraham was pleading with God during that trip to make another way, if possible, provide another sacrifice. As Abraham raised the knife to slay his son, an angel ordered Abraham not to hurt Isaac. At that moment, Abraham heard a noise. He turned and looked and saw the answer to his prayer. A ram was caught in a bush, and once again, God, with his perfect timing, provided an answer. Abraham took the ram from the bush and sacrificed it on the altar instead of his son Isaac. God answered Abraham's prayer when he provided another source for sacrifice.

Now about the question I raised earlier of how we know if it is God's will that a mother, father, sibling, or a grandparent be saved. To answer that question, we must know what God has to say about it in his word. Remember, in the introduction, I stated that the purpose of writing this book was threefold: (1) to give hope to believers concerning their unsaved loved ones, (2) to give hope to those who are bound by addiction, especially alcohol, and (3) to instruct believers on how to pray for the unsaved and see the salvation of their loved ones come to pass. I realize this is a bold statement, so let me show it to you in the Word.

All the forces of hell cannot stop the answer to our prayers when we pray in the will of God. Answers may be delayed by Satan's forces or sometimes slowed down by God's own timing. Our enemies are not the neighbors, not our spouses, and not the crazy drivers on the road. Our enemies are the demonic forces that attempt to hold the world in captivity with unbelief and evil. But our spiritual weapons are prayer, intercessions, giving of thanks, and preaching the Word of God. Ephesians 6:12 states, "For we wrestle not against flesh and blood…"

So again, I ask, What is God's will for your unsaved family members? First Peter 3:9 answers the question, "Who will have all men to be saved and none perish?" "God's will or desire is for all men to be saved and come to the knowledge of the truth." This is the *predicate* that must be established in our hearts and minds when we pray for a loved one's salvation. My goal is to stretch and build up your faith when you pray for your loved ones.

Now with this knowledge in our hearts, you and I can lift the name of our family member up to the throne room of God and present them to our heavenly Father. We can ask him with confidence to bring that loved one into salvation in the name of Jesus Christ. First John 5:14–15 states, "And this is the confidence that we have in Him, that, if we ask anything according to His will, he heareth us and if we know that he hears us, whatsoever we ask, we know that we have the petitions that we desired of him." Our prayers become effective when we pray in the will of God.

When we pray according to the will of God, all heaven moves in behalf of our prayers. We are then in agreement with his word. Have faith in God's word and his promises. Jesus walked by faith, lived by faith, died by faith, and rose from hell and the grave by faith. He taught us that prayer is the key to heaven, but having faith and believing in his word are what really counts because faith unlocks the door to heaven. Doubt short-circuits our prayers and hinders the answer to our petitions. Doubt creates a distraction from the word of faith and from the promises of God that are "Yeah" and "Amen." In Mark 11:24, Jesus tells us, "Therefore I say unto you what things so ever you desire, when you pray, believe that you receive, and you shall have them." We haven't finished praying until we, by faith, believe that we have received the answer to our petition. I encourage you to stop trying to earn the promises of God. Just receive them by faith. Stagger not at the promises of God.

The God kind of faith is believing without seeing; our faith is not in what we see or feel. Faith and hope are what I call the power twins. But the God kind of faith changes hope into reality. Believing you have received without seeing an instant manifestation is faith in action. St. Paul stated that faith is all the substance we need. The God kind of faith calls things that are not as though they are. St. Paul said that faith is giving substance to things hoped for. Jesus said, "Blessed are they that have not seen me and yet have believed."

When praying for something, don't just hope that God will answer your prayer. Hope speaks of the future or looks to future events of something good coming to pass. When you say "I hope this will happen," you are expecting something in the future to take place. But faith is in the present, the here and now. Faith speaks to the present. When you pray believing that you have received the answer to your request, that is faith in action.

If we want to know how to pray accurately and effectively, then we must know what the Master has said about prayer. For too long, many Christians have thought they could pray any way they want and to whomever they want, not considering what God's Word has to say about prayer—prayer that brings results. There is a prayer that tears down spiritual strongholds, delivers people out of Satan's hand, and gives them eternal life.

Jesus said in John 16:23, "And in that day you shall ask me nothing. Verily, verily, I say unto you, whatsoever you ask the Father in my name, He will give it you." Christ is saying "in that day" after he ascends into heaven and sits at the right hand of the Father, he will be your advocate, your intercessor, and your high priest. And when you pray to the Father, in his name, it will be done. Jesus further instructed us in John 14:13–14, "And whatsoever you shall ask in my name, that will I do, that the Father may be glorified in the Son. If you ask anything in my name, I will do it." There is power in the sovereign name of Jesus Christ. Jesus possesses the supreme and ultimate power in his creation.

How many times have we heard Christians pray to the Spirit, to dead saints, or even to idols? It should not be a mystery why so many prayers are not answered. It is the name of Jesus Christ that delivers our prayers into the throne room of God. Christ told us in John 16:26 (KJV), "At that day you shall ask in my name, and I say not unto you, that I will pray the Father for you." Jesus is not only our high priest who is ever making intercession for us but also our mediator, declaring to the heavenly Father that we are one of his and that we belong to the heavenly family.

Believing is the key to answered prayer. Jesus declared in Matthew 21:22, "And all things whatsoever you shall ask in prayer, believing, you shall receive." The word *whatsoever* includes praying for the deliverance and salvation of your friends and family. When you pray for them, declare and prophesy deliverance and salvation over them in the name of Jesus Christ. Many Christians find it difficult to pray for the salvation of their family and really believe that they will be saved. Why should our prayers for the unsaved be any different from when we pray for the healing of our sick bodies? Once again, we haven't finished praying until we believe, by faith, that we have received the answer to our prayers.

The book of James instructs us to be specific in our prayers. James 4:3 says, "You ask and receive not, because you ask amiss." *Webster's Dictionary* defines the word *amiss* as "asking for something inappropriately, or out of place." When I was growing up, we always had Thanksgiving dinner at my aunt's house. We would gather around the table, and my aunt would usually pray for five minutes or more before we would eat. During her long prayer, I would open one eye and look at the hot turkey and gravy and watch them getting cold. I would think, *Please Lord, make her stop praying so we can eat.* She would pray for all the missionaries around the world. Then she would bring the prayer back to the United States and would pray for her church and all the unsaved people in town, and often she would forget to bless the food. This is praying amiss!

The Word teaches us to be specific in our prayers and doubt not. James 1:6 states, "But let him ask in faith, without doubting, for one who doubts is tossed about." Doubt is the opposite of faith. It creates a distraction from the promises of God. Doubt short-circuits our faith and will hinder the answers to your prayers. Doubt will prevent you from moving mountains in your life. Jesus told us, "If we have faith, we can say to the mountain be thou removed, and it shall be moved!" (Matthew 17:20).

PART TWO
PRAYING FOR THE UNSAVED

One of the biggest challenges in our life is to really believe for the deliverance and salvation of a loved one. I know how painful it is to watch someone you love circle the drain in life, and as time goes by, see alcoholism make them sicker and fill them with despair and become more despondent to their family and the Lord. But I have witnessed my unsaved loved ones be delivered and saved and become new creatures in Christ through authoritative and accurate prayer. St. Paul said in Ephesians 3:20, "Now unto him that is able to do exceedingly abundantly above all that we ask or think, according to the power that worketh in us." What is that power St. Paul is speaking of that works within us? We are told in 2 Timothy 1:7, "For God has not given us the spirit of fear, but of love, power, and a sound mind."

If we have the authority, as a believer, to cast our devils in the name of Jesus, from where does that authority come? Our authority as a believer comes from the mouth of Jesus. In Mark 16:17–18, Jesus said, "And these signs shall follow them that believe, in my name shall they cast our devils; they shall speak with new tongues; they shall take up serpents; and if they drink any deadly thing, it shall not hurt them; they shall lay hands on the sick, and they shall recover." My friends, there it is! He has given us believers authority to do his work in his name.

Jesus Christ himself gave us the authority to cast out demons and pray for the sick and see them healed. As believers, we need a demonstration of the power and authority of God in our lives and in our churches. When a loved one is bound by the devil because of alcoholism or other substances, we have the authority from and by the name of Jesus Christ to command Satan to release them and set them free. We don't command Jesus to do anything. We command Satan to get out. We dismiss sickness in the name of Jesus Christ. Christ has vested within us his love, his power, his authority, his wisdom, and his inheritance. What Jesus has been given, he has given to us. He is even preparing beautiful, heavenly homes for us called mansions. Remember, Jesus was a finished carpenter, and our heavenly homes will be more magnificent that we can imagine. I know you want your loved ones to have a home in heaven. Maybe their mansions will be next to yours (Galatians 4: 6–7).

Before you pray a prayer of deliverance and salvation over anyone, invite two other faith-filled believers to join you in prayer. In Matthew 18:18, Jesus taught us, "Whatever you bind on earth shall be bound in heaven, and whatsoever you loose on earth shall be loosed in heaven." In verse 19, he instructs us, "Again I say unto you that if any two of you shall agree on earth as touching anything that they shall ask, it shall be done for them of my Father which is in heaven. For where two or three are gathered together in my name, there am I in the midst of them." There is power in agreement when we pray together. This is what those young believers did so many years ago when they prayed and commanded Satan to release my Dad, to take the blinders off his eyes in the name of Jesus Christ, and to set him free so Dad could see and hear the Word of God and respond to Christ's calling. They operated in the authority that Jesus had given to them as believers. Guess what? It worked! There is *power* in the *sovereign name of Jesus Christ*!

In Mark 11:24, Jesus said, "What things soever you desire, when you pray, believe that you receive them, and you shall have them." If we don't operate in Mark 11:24 when we pray, are we ignoring the scriptures? The above scripture is a promise from Jesus. If my dad being human could keep his promises, how much more faithful is God in keeping his?

A person can think themselves to death with doubt, worry, and negative thoughts. We need to lose our minds and gain the mind of Christ. The mind of Christ says if you believe, if you will really believe that you receive, and not doubt, you will have what you asked. (Caveat! I have never seen God answer a selfish prayer with a yes.) We must renew our thinking and renew our minds with the Word of God. We cannot come to God with doubt and unbelief, then expect a miracle. Remember, faith unlocks the door to the throne room of God.

When we pray in the will of God, the angels stand with their wings unfolded, ready to swoop down and bring the answer to our prayers. They will fight off the demons as they did for Daniel when he prayed for understanding. The demons were attempting to hinder the answer to Daniel's prayer. But the angels intervened, and Daniel received his answer.

When those young Christians prayed for my father's deliverance, they did not stop there. They prayed for his salvation and, by faith, claimed him to the kingdom of God. Remember what Jesus said in Mark 11:23–24, "What things soever you desire, when you pray, believe that you receive them, and you shall have them." Note that Jesus did not say except when you pray for the salvation of a family member or friend. We haven't finished praying until we believe we have received (Mark 11:24). Earlier, I established a predicate, a truth that God's will is that all men would be saved and none would perish. Therefore, when we pray for the salvation of an individual, we are praying in the will of God. When we pray in God's will, all heaven gets into action to bring the answer to fruition. It's like pulling a fire alarm or calling 911; here come the angels! All heaven responds and gets into action. Remember, answers to our prayers are released in God's perfect timing. After you have prayed and believed for their salvation, it is paramount that you ask the heavenly Father to send a messenger with the gospel of grace into their lives.

Psalm 107:20 says, "He sent his word and healed them and delivered them from their destructions." Don't limit God with the negative words about your unsaved loved ones. After you have prayed for their salvation by faith, see them as saved. Form a mental picture of the people you have claimed to the kingdom, confessing Jesus as Lord. Speak words of spiritual life over them; prophesy that they will know Jesus Christ as Savior and that they will make heaven their home. Even the Old Testament promises believers that their offspring shall not be destroyed. Proverbs 11:21 says, "The seed of the righteous shall be delivered."

Some of you reading this may be asking, "Where in the Bible does it say I can prophesy salvation over a friend or loved one?" I'm glad you asked! The answer is found in Acts 16. Paul and Silas were arrested and brought to the city square where they were severely beaten. After the beating, Paul and Silas were thrown into prison where their feet were placed in stocks. At midnight, Paul and Silas prayed and sang praises unto God, and the prisoners and the jailer heard them (verse 25). Suddenly, there was a great earthquake. And all the doors were opened, and everyone's stocks were loosed (verse 26). The jailer who was ordered to keep Paul and Silas in safe custody was about to kill himself when Paul cried out, "Do yourself no harm. We are all here!" Then the jailer brought them out of the innermost part of the prison and asked, "Sirs, what must I do to be saved?"

Did Paul tell the jailer he must join the local church and become a member in good standing, then he would be saved? Of course not! Paul said in Acts 16:31, "Believe on the Lord Jesus Christ, and thou shall be saved." But notice Paul did not stop there. Paul included the jailer's family by prophesying, "And all thy house" (verse 21). Verse 32 tells us they spoke unto the jailer the Word of the Lord and to all who were in the jailer's house. In verse 33, the jailer, the same hour of the night, washed the disciple's wounds, and the jailer and his whole family were baptized. After the family believed and were baptized, the jailer prepared a meal for Paul, Silas, and his family; and together they all rejoiced, believing in God. What I want you to glean from this is that Paul prophesied that the jailer's family, all of them, would be saved, and it came to pass. Within hours, the whole family accepted Christ as Savior, and they fellowshipped together, worshipping God.

After praying for that unsaved loved one and claiming them to the kingdom of God, believe by faith that you receive the answer to that prayer. Proclaim it, sing about it, shout about it, thank God for it, prophesy as Paul did, and believe it will happen. The answer to that prayer is coming. It's on the way. It will come to pass. Have faith in God's promise that they will, in God's timing, accept Jesus Christ as Savior. By faith, call things that are not as though they are! If you prayed in faith, believing that your family member will accept Christ, do not pray that same prayer of salvation for them again. For we have this confidence that if we pray in the will of God, we know that he heard us; and if we know that he heard us, we know that we have the answer to our petitions.

I believe there may be a few people reading this who still are not convinced that they can or should prophesy salvation over their unsaved loved ones. Acts 2:17 says, "And it shall come to pass in the last days, saith God, I will pour out of my Spirit upon all flesh and your sons and daughters shall prophesy." Proverbs 18:21 says, "Life and death are in the power of the tongue." We can't speak words of unbelief or words of death and expect life to come forth. Earlier in the book, I admonished Christians to never confess that their loved ones are hopeless cases spiritually and that they probably will go to hell. In John 6:68, Peter told Jesus, "You have the words that give eternal life." When we made Jesus Christ Lord and Savior of our lives, he put his spirit and words of life into our hearts. So now we can give his words of life to others.

Years ago, someone said, "My brother is so far in the gutter, so evil that hell wouldn't even want him." Please seal this truth in your heart: there isn't one person who is so sinful that God cannot reach him or her. Ephesians 5:26 says that "We are sanctified and cleansed with the washing of water by the word." Reading and hearing the Word of God has a cleansing effect on our soul and body. No matter how low a person has sunk into decadence, God's word will still reach them. Water always flows to the lowest level, and the washing of the water of God's word will reach an unsaved individual no matter how low they have fallen.

Faith in Action

We are told in James 2:26, "For as the body without the Spirit is dead, so faith without works is dead also." Some Christians believe James is saying that in order to be saved, we must not only accept Jesus as Savior but also perform good deeds. In other words, it's belief in Jesus plus performance of righteous acts that secure a place in heaven. This is contrary to all Paul's writings. The formula for salvation is not Jesus plus works plus something else. The equation for receiving salvation is Jesus plus nothing else equals everything—eternal life. It is Christ's performance, what he did at Calvary, that secures my salvation, not my performance here on earth. When James said, "Faith without works is dead," he was saying faith without corresponding action or faith without results is dead. We put our faith into action when we really believe God's promises and receive them by faith in the name of Jesus Christ. This is faith in action—believing before receiving. We are promised in Luke 1:37, "For with God nothing shall be impossible." Again, I say, stagger not at the promises of God. Hebrews 10:23 (KJV) states: "Let us hold fast the profession of our faith without wavering; (for he is faithful that promised;)…"

Answered Prayer

Several years ago, I preached in a revival meeting in North Platt, Nebraska. On the last night of the revival, I spoke on how to pray for the unsaved and see them saved. At the end of the message, people came forward to the altar to pray for their unsaved loved ones. A boy, about ten years old, came up to me with tears in his eyes. He looked up at me and asked me to pray for his sister. He wanted her to know Jesus as her personal Savior. I had special empathy for that young boy, as I knew how he felt. When I was his age, I desperately wanted my dad to be saved. The little boy gave me his sister's name, and together we lifted up his sister by name to the throne room of God. His sister did not have any addictions to any substances, such as alcohol or drugs. What she needed was salvation. Together we claimed her to the kingdom of God and proclaimed salvation over her life in the name of Jesus Christ. Then we asked the heavenly Father to send a messenger with the gospel of grace to his sister. After the prayer, I assured the boy that God had heard our prayer and that he would someday see his sister born again and confess Jesus as Lord of her life. I now realize that what I did was prophesy that his sister would someday be born again. The service concluded at about 9:00 p.m., and I returned to my hotel room.

Early the next morning, I received a call from Pastor Bob from the church. He apologized for calling so early but said what he had to share couldn't wait. He asked if I remembered the young boy's sister that we prayed for last evening. I replied, "Of course."

Pastor Bob continued, "Last night, while we were in the service, two of our members were going door to door in an apartment complex, talking to people about the love of God. It was about 9:30 p.m., and one of the witnesses said, 'It's getting late. Maybe we should quit for the night.' But then they decided to knock on one more apartment door, and guess who opened the door? It was the little boy's sister. She invited them in, and within minutes, she prayed and received Jesus Christ as her Savior."

Isn't that wonderful! Within one hour after praying for that young lady, she was born again and now has a home in heaven for eternity. God honored our prayer and sent two messengers with the gospel of grace to that young woman. In no way do I take credit for that woman's salvation experience. All the glory goes to Jesus Christ who set into motion the events that led to her becoming a born-again child of God. A group of believers simply prayed according to the Word of God as Jesus had instructed, and the Holy Spirit did the rest. In prayer, tear down those spiritual walls and pray against the evil forces that are holding your loved ones in captivity and claim them to the kingdom of God in the name of Jesus.

A few months later, I was speaking in a church in Oklahoma City, Oklahoma. I spoke on how to pray for the deliverance and salvation of the unsaved. At the end of the service, a couple came up to the altar for prayer. Tearfully they asked me to pray for their teenage son who had disappeared with several friends when he was fourteen. They had not heard from him since he ran away. I felt the Lord prompt me to pray for his deliverance from drugs, and then we all prayed for him to be saved and claimed him to the kingdom of God. We asked the Lord to send a messenger with the message of grace to this young man.

About three months later, the pastor from Oklahoma City called and shared the following story about the teenage son we had prayed for:

I don't remember the young man's name, but let's call him Ted. Ted had been traveling with his friends in a van for about eighteen months, doing illegal drugs, scavenging for food, and occasionally stealing items they needed. One day, they stopped somewhere in Wyoming to beg for food and money. While Ted's friends were attempting to get food, something came over Ted. He decided he

PART TWO
PRAYING FOR THE UNSAVED

had had enough of the drug-filled life and of living as a homeless person. When his friends were not watching, Ted slipped away. Ted aimlessly wandered through the streets of the city until he found a telephone booth. He turned to the yellow pages of the directory and found the name of a Baptist pastor. When the pastor answered his call, Ted told him how he had been living for the past one and a half years and that he wanted to go home. The pastor immediately picked Ted up and took him to his church office, where the pastor then led him to Jesus Christ in prayer. Ted then called his parents and told them how he had been living and that he wanted to come home. I can only imagine the joy that flooded their hearts when they received that call from their son Ted, who had been lost but now was found. Not only was Ted found but was also born again, safe, and on his way home to Oklahoma. God ordered all those events to come together to reach Ted as a result of fervent, accurate, and authoritative prayer. All praise and glory to the Lord of heaven.

I was scheduled to speak in a church in Gainesville, Georgia, for three services. My singers, the Chapel Trio, traveled with me most of the time. Alma Lee, our alto singer, was invited to stay with the pastor and his family, while my wife and I stayed in a local hotel. The next morning was Sunday, and all of us met for prayer before the service. What Alma told me that morning made me have goose bumps on my arm. The pastor and his wife had a sixteen-year-old daughter, and Alma was going to use their daughter's bedroom for three nights. Alma informed me that there was a figurine or statue of a black snake curled up as though it was ready to strike mounted above the headboard, looking down at her. Alma then described some of the satanic symbols and artifacts placed throughout the bedroom. The pastor's daughter was totally involved in witchcraft. I now knew why we were sent to minister in this fellowship.

For the next three nights, I stood flat-footed and preached my heart out, praying that the gospel would touch their daughter's heart. During the final service, the pastor's daughter and her boyfriend sat in the back of the church, laughing and talking as I spoke, which was somewhat disruptive. The satanic forces that surrounded their daughter and her boyfriend were palatable.

The next morning, we were leaving Gainesville, and all of us decided we could not leave without praying deliverance over that teenage daughter. Stan Way, our guitarist, led in prayer. We prayed as Jesus had taught us, commanding Satan to turn her loose and set her free in the name of Jesus. Then we prayed and claimed this girl to the kingdom of God, asking and believing that she would someday confess Jesus as her Lord and Savior.

After staying on the road, singing, and preaching for several more weeks, we returned to Phoenix, Arizona, where we all lived. After a few days resting at home, we left again for another tour; this time, without Stan. Several weeks had passed when I received a call from Stan. His voice was filled with excitement as he shared the good news. The pastor's daughter that we had earnestly prayed for weeks earlier had been delivered from satanism and witchcraft, and she had accepted Jesus as her Savior. What a victory! God had honored his word, and all glory goes to him.

I want to share one more story of victory. The Trio and I were ministering in a church in High Point, North Carolina. We were scheduled for two services, one in the morning and one in the evening. I did not teach how to pray for the salvation of your loved ones during the morning service. I simply shared the endless grace of Jesus Christ and then gave a simple altar call. There was a man sitting with his family about four rows from the front. This gentleman responded to the invitation to receive Jesus as his Savior.

After the morning service, we joined Pastor Dan Duncan for lunch, and he shared that the man who prayed to receive Jesus as Lord rarely ever came to the church except for Christmas programs. Pastor then shared that the man's family had earnestly been praying for their father for several years. Apparently, the man's wife had learned how to pray for the unsaved by studying what the Bible had to say about using your faith when praying for someone's salvation. His wife prayed for his salvation years earlier and, by faith, claimed him to Jesus Christ for salvation and believed she received the answer to her prayer. Obviously, I'm not the only believer who has discovered what the Bible has to say about praying for the unsaved.

On Sunday night, the new convert and his family attended the service. Just before I spoke, that man stood up and gave a testimony of his salvation experience that set that congregation on fire with praise to God. I thought that I was listening to a man who had studied the Bible for several years. He shared with the church that after he prayed for salvation in the morning service, he went home, had lunch with his family, and started reading the New Testament. He studied the gospels for nearly five hours before coming to the evening service. This convert talked about the shedding of Christ's incorruptible blood and the grace of Jesus Christ like he was a seasoned preacher.

This is what happens when we take God's word seriously and pray in the manner that Jesus has taught. When you pray, believe that you receive the requests you have made known to the heavenly Father, and you shall have them (Mark 11:24). Spiritual weapons of warfare, in both the New and Old Testament, describe the many spiritual weapons that are available to us that will defeat the attacks of the enemy every time. Ephesians 6:14 charges us to "stand therefore, having your loins girt about you with truth, and having on the breastplate of righteousness, and your feet shod with the preparation of the gospel of peace; above all, taking the shield of faith..." The foregoing are powerful spiritual weapons of warfare, and they work when we operate in them. I discussed at length 1 Timothy 2:1 that exhorts us to exercise different types of prayer, which include: (1) supplications (prayers for specific needs), (2) prayers (words of worship, confessions, and praises to God), (3) intercessions (to pray in behalf of others, which I will discuss later), and (4) giving of thanks (praising God with a thankful heart). These are just some of our spiritual weapons in God's arsenal that bring healing, deliverance, salvation, and victory over the wiles of the devil. Nothing in this world can stand against or penetrate the Shekinah glory of God. Those fiery darts never get to our spirit or soul. When they hit the shield of faith, they are extinguished; they disappear into his Shekinah glory. The same fate awaits for Satan and all the scoffers and haters of Jesus after the final judgment. They will be consumed in the starburst, the Shekinah glory of God. What happens to any object that falls into the sun? That object is consumed, and it is as though it never existed.

But good news, we who are born again will live and thrive for eternity in Christ—our bright and morning star.

The word *Shekinah* is a Hebrew word that means "the one who dwells." The word *Shekinah* refers to "the personal presence of God among his people." It is the radiance and glory of God. When we are born again, Jesus takes up residence within us. Jesus confirmed this in John 15:17 when he declared, "If you abide in me, and my words abide in you, you shall ask what you will and it shall be done unto you." I did not make this up; these words are from the mouth of Jesus Christ.

After you have prayed, create a visual picture of your prayers being answered. Words that come from our mouth matter. The scriptures tell us that we can be trapped by our words. Proverbs 6:2 says, "Thou art snared with the words of thy mouth, thou art taken with the words of thy mouth." Satan doesn't want us to speak words of life, of healing, and of salvation. The enemy throws all types of situations and negative words at us, attempting to distract us from speaking words of faith. One of our spiritual weapons is speaking the Word of God into every situation we encounter. The Word of God tells us that faith comes by hearing the Word of God, but our faith is also increased by revelation. The dictionary defines the word *revelation* as "a surprising and previously unknown fact, especially one that is made known in a dramatic way." It also means "the divine discloser to man of something relating to God's promises." I believe that this teaching on prayer and faith is becoming a revelation to many.

I have preached in many different Baptist organizations and other churches. Almost every denomination has embraced this teaching on faith and on how to pray for the unsaved, and they have seen miracles of salvation happen for their family members. Like my dad, many of those who became born again were called hopeless cases, spiritually. Sadly, some friends said to me, "Gary, this may give false hope to people and create disappointment." I answer that question with a question. Won't a family member be disappointed and saddened if their loved one dies without Jesus because they never prayed with faith, believing that that loved one would be saved? Of course, they would. What do you have to lose by praying with authority and claiming that person to the kingdom of God, by faith, in Jesus's name? Paul wrote in 1 Timothy 1:7, "For God has not given us the Spirit of fear, but of power, and of love, and of a sound mind." Also, I highly suggest that every believer read Romans 8:15 every day and reassure yourself that you have been adopted into the heavenly family by our heavenly Father through Jesus Christ our Lord. Paul taught us, "For you have received the Spirit of adoption, whereby we cry, Abba Father."

Earlier in this book, I wrote that as believers, Jesus has given us what he has been given (John 14:12, 17:22). We have been given his power to overcome Satan's attacks and temptations and the power to be witnesses for him throughout this world. In Acts 1:8, we are told that we will receive power when the Holy Spirit has come on us and that we will be his witnesses in Jerusalem and to the end of the earth.

Love

When we are born again, Jesus takes up residence within us. He dwells with us. We become one—Christ in us and we in him (John 17:21–23). When God moves into your life, he will not move out because you made a mistake or sinned. God has promised that he will never leave or forsake you. God has the sovereignty to do what he wishes, except violate his own words (promises) or to lie. We are God's dwelling place, and he will not change addresses (2 Corinthians 6:16). God's dwells in our hearts by faith (Ephesians 3:17).

Born-again believers, you are now one of his sheep, forever. Now *this* is good news! He is a jealous God, and he will never let you go. What blessed comfort we can find in Isaiah 43:25 which says, "I, even I, am he that blotteth out thy transgressions for mine own sake, and will not remember thy sins."

Christ in us is the hope of glory. Now I can say with confidence, since Christ is within me, the faith and love of Christ also dwell within me. Since we are in Christ, we have the character of Jesus within us. We have his love, his power, his wisdom, and yes, his faith. Faith and love are found in Jesus Christ (1 Timothy 1:14; John 5:5). Faith and love seem to be synonymous; they certainly do work together. Paul wrote in 1 Timothy 1:14, "And the grace of our Lord was exceedingly abundant with faith and love which is in Christ Jesus." Since we have the love of God abiding in us, we can ask the heavenly Father to manifest or to bring forth the love of Jesus that is within us. God has sent us a helper, the Holy Spirit, to release the love of Jesus that abides within. Romans 5:5 says, "Because the love of God is shed abroad in our hearts by the Holy Ghost which is given unto us."

It is paramount that we understand Galations 5:6, which says, "Faith worketh by love." I believe Paul is warning us that if we do not operate and walk in love, our prayers will be hindered, because faith pours out of the spirit of love. We are told in Mark 11:25, "And when you stand praying, forgive, if you have unforgiveness against any." Faith will not flow or work from a bitter, unforgiving heart. Since faith works by love and we have the love of Christ within us, we thereby can walk in the Master's love. Love covers all sins (Proverbs 10:12). Paul told us to love by faith. In Ephesians 6:23, he said, "Peace be to the brethren, and love with faith, from God the Father and the Lord Jesus Christ." We have all met or known people who are unlovable. It is not easy to love someone who is hard to reach. They will act as though they don't need love or affection and won't allow anyone to get close. This type of person desperately needs our love. Paul said we can love others by faith (Ephesians 6:23). The following is how I pray for that type of individual:

Heavenly Father, I confess that your love is within me, and I ask that your spirit of love will constantly flow from me to that individual. By faith, I proclaim that I love them as Christ loves me, in the name of Jesus.

A Sound Mind

A sound mind is a mind that is healthy and disciplined and that operates in self-control. At first blush, it is easy to interpret the word *self-control* to mean we have to do something about our crazy thoughts and negative behaviors. But wouldn't that be self-righteousness? Focus on the word *spirit* in 2 Timothy 1:7, which says, "He has given us a spirit of a sound mind." We operate with a sound mind by constantly relying on the grace of God that has been given to us by and through Jesus Christ. Like our gift of salvation, a sound mind is also a gift from the Lord. I can only walk with a disciplined mind when I put my faith totally in him.

When I was a teenager, I never looked forward to the New Year's Eve service at church. The youth minister would tell us to list all our sins on a sheet of paper, place the paper in an envelope, and wait one year before opening it. In the following year, we were to pray and ask the Lord to help us reduce or eliminate our sin list. Well, my list was rather long, and after waiting one year, I opened the envelope and reviewed that old sin list. As I read that old list, I became very discouraged. Not only had I not shortened last year's list but I also had to add more sins to that list. Thank God for his grace that comes from Jesus Christ. "Where sin abounded, grace much more did abound" (Romans 5:20).

After a couple of years, I became frustrated with my sin lists. I saw the futility in trying to make myself righteous by shortening or reducing my sins. After several years of feeling that I was constantly disappointing the Lord, at the age of twenty, I stopped trying to change and reduce my sins. I didn't give up on Jesus. I gave up on myself. While growing up, I was repeatedly told by preachers that even though we had accepted Jesus as our Savior, we were still walking a tight rope or were on a high wire spiritually throughout our life. We were instructed that heaven was on the right side and that hell was on the left, and we wouldn't know which side we would fall on, heaven or hell, until we died. This is spiritual insecurity. Tell your family and friends that when you are saved in Christ, nothing can separate you from the love of God. Paul, in the Epistles, told us that when we are saved, we are in the hand of God, and guess what God is doing with his other hand? God is covering his hand that holds all his adopted children. We are thereby covered and sealed in the hands of God. Neither the devil nor any of his demons can pry open God's hands and pluck us out (John 10:29).

It is imperative that you read Romans 8:35–39, which says that nothing can separate us from the love of God. In summary, Paul declares that neither death, nor life, nor things to come, nor height, nor depth, nor any creature can separate us from the love of God. I ask, Are you a creature? Are you strong enough to pry yourself out of the hand of God? I don't believe you are and neither am I. When we become one of Christ's sheep, he will never let us go. I mentioned earlier that I became discouraged with the teaching of the church, and at the age of twenty, I stopped fellowshipping with the church and with Jesus. And here is the reason: After years of being told that I wouldn't know if I made heaven or hell until I died and being made to feel that I was a failure and that I could be saved today and lost tomorrow, I gave up.

Through the years, I have heard Christians testify that they had been saved all their lives and that they would only make heaven if they were faithful until the last moment. What does that even mean? This is eternal insecurity. That statement reeks of self-righteousness. German shepherds are more faithful to their masters than Christians are to one another and to the Master. Our salvation is not about us; it is all about him and his performance at Calvary that gives us eternal life. Christ's faithfulness and righteousness are imputed to us who are redeemed through his blood. Jesus is the true and faithful witness. When you make Jesus Lord of your life, you have an inseparable eternal relationship with him with the heavenly Father and all heaven. St. Paul declared, with confidence, "For I know whom I have believed, and am persuaded that he is able to keep that which I have committed unto him against that day" (2 Timothy 1:12). Paul reaffirms this truth in Philippians 1:6 with surety by writing, "Being confident of this very thing, that he which hath begun a good work in you will perform it until the day of Jesus Christ." Have faith in Christ's promises to keep you and to conform you into his image by the working of the Holy Spirit until Jesus returns. "Line upon line, precept upon precept, He is changing me." He will never give up on you. You belong to him. He will fight for you and will never let you go. I implore you to have faith in Christ's promises to keep you, to complete you, and to hold you forever in the palm of his hand. If you wander away from the sheepfold and become lost, Jesus, our Good Shepherd, will find you and carry you back home. This is the assurance and confidence that we have in him. It is a promise from Jesus Christ which has been sealed with his precious blood.

The Good Shepherd

I want to discuss the love of the Good Shepherd found in Luke 15:4. It may appear that I'm starting a new subject, and you may be thinking, *What does this have to do with faith or my salvation?* The story of the Good Shepherd has everything to do with faith and eternal life. Some reading this teaching may be struggling with believing that they are really saved and secured in the arms of Jesus forevermore. I wrote earlier, while growing up, I rarely felt safe and secure concerning my salvation. I wanted to feel something. I wanted to feel righteous, but instead I lived with the fear that I may not make heaven. I used my sin list as a measuring stick to determine how righteous I was becoming. If I shortened my sin list, I felt more righteous. This self-righteous thinking and behavior created spiritual uncertainty and major anxiety. We are not saved by feelings. We are saved by grace through faith and not of ourselves (Ephesians 2:8). If you have received Jesus Christ as your Lord and confessed him as your Savior, you will never be more saved than you are right now! Paul said in Romans 1:17, "But the righteous shall live by faith." First Peter 1:21 tells us that our faith and hope are in God. Our salvation is not secured by ourselves; it is given to us as a gift by what Jesus did on the cross. It is all about him! It is Christ's performance and his obedience to his heavenly Father that redeem us and open heaven's doors for you and me.

The parable of the lost sheep is found in Luke 15, where Jesus told the story of a man who had one hundred sheep, and for some reason, one of the sheep wandered away from the fold and became lost. Jesus, being the good shepherd, left the ninety-nine and searched until he found the lost sheep. When he found it, he put it on his shoulders and carried it home; and when he arrived, his friends and neighbors rejoiced with him. It is important to note that the lost sheep was one of the one hundred sheep in the sheepfold. That lost sheep belonged to Jesus, the Shepherd. Like that one sheep, I left the fellowship of the fold and became lost in the wilderness. But one night, while staying in a friend's cabin in Opal Mountain, the Good Shepherd showed up. He reestablished and restored me, and I then knew how much Jesus really loved me. Did I repent? Of course! *Webster's Dictionary* says to repent is to change your mind about God. I repented for doubting that the Lord could really save me and hold me in his hand forever. Whatever is not of faith is sin (Romans 14:23). I repented for the negative thoughts I had about God and forgave the Bible teachers for instilling in me a gospel of legalism and self-righteousness. That night at Opal Mountain, I changed my mind about God and have never doubted him again.

The Good Shepherd's Prayer for Us

The Lord's priestly prayer for his disciples, for you and me, is found in John 17. In this chapter, Jesus reveals his love for us and discloses what our future is and will be in him. In this prayer, Christ seals us with God and himself. The following is a summary of Christ's high priestly prayer for himself and for all who believe:

In his prayer, Jesus declared that all the believers whom God has given him belong to him and to God. Jesus prayed, "Holy Father, keep through thine own name those whom you have given me, that they may be one, as we are" (verse 11). Jesus, in his prayer, announced that "I have kept all of those that you gave me, and none of them is lost" (verse 12). But Jesus did not stop there; in verse 20, Jesus included you and me. Jesus prayed, "Neither pray I for these alone, but for them also which shall believe on me through their word, that they all may be one, as thou, Father, art in me, and I in thee, that they also may be one is us" (verse 21).

Do you believe that God has answered and will continue to answer his son's prayer? In verse 21, we are told that Christ is one with God. When we are in Jesus, we are not only one with him but also one with God forever! I sincerely ask, Do you see what the Lord is telling us? Our salvation and eternal life were secured in him because of what he did at Calvary, not by what we can do. The Word of God tells us that the blood of Jesus Christ cleanses us from all unrighteousness. Now that I am born again, my life and soul are under the blood of Jesus. I am covered—yes, covered—with the sin-

69

less, incorruptible blood of Jesus Christ. Now when God looks at me, he no longer sees my sin, my failures, and my faults; he sees the blood of his dear son that covers me for eternity.

I'm going to share a story that illustrates the above teaching. Several years ago, a friend of mine gave me an eleven-year-old Lincoln Town Car. It was beautiful for its age, and it was over eighteen-feet long. The car was nearly as big as the first apartment I had while going to college. One morning, as I walked toward the car, I noticed scratches on the two doors on the driver's side. The scratches were in circles as though someone used a nail or key to make them. I bought car polish, and after buffing out those marks, the doors looked fine. A few days passed, and as I approached the car, I saw that those same scratches had reappeared. I thought, *What in the world is happening?* So I got the polish and again buffed out those scratches, and when I finished, I didn't see any marks. Well, I think you can guess what happened a few days later. As I walked toward the car, once again, those scratches reappeared on the car doors. I then realized what the car needed was a new paint job. This is what Jesus does for the sinner. When people come to the Lord for salvation, they come to him with damage that has resulted from sin and separation from God. When the blood of Jesus covers an individual, all the marks and stains of sin and imperfections are gone; it's as though they never existed (2 Corinthians 5:17–18). Jesus himself told us, "My Father, which gave them me, is greater than all; and no man is able to pluck them out of my Father's hand"(John 10:29). God himself has declared, "Behold, I have graven thee upon the palms of my hands: thy walls are continually before me" (Isaiah 49:16). Graven means God has written our names into his palms. Isn't that wonderful! God's promise of salvation and preservation to Israel is given to us by adoption through the new blood covenant of grace. When we became born again, we became new creatures in Christ. We who believe Jesus is our Savior have an inseparable, eternal relationship with the Lord of heaven. We have been adopted by agape love through Jesus Christ and are a part of God's heavenly kingdom. This is part of the good news to all creation. My hope is that you who are redeemed by the blood of Jesus will share this good news at every opportunity.

Faith

God has given every person a measure of faith (Romans 12:13), and we increase that measure of faith by reading and hearing the Word of God (Romans 10:17). We are forever increasing our faith; it never stops growing until we are face-to-face with Jesus. Jesus Christ is the author and perfecter of our faith (Hebrews 12:2). We are told in 1 Peter 1:21 that God raised Jesus from the dead and gave him glory, and our faith and hope are now in God. Our faith increases as we step out into the deep waters, putting and keeping our trust and faith in him.

Faith is also increased when we experience dark moments of sadness and are sorely tested. When we walk through the shadowy valley of death, we are not alone. We quickly discover Christ is walking with us and has been leading us all the time. In the midst of the dark valley, if we listen, we will hear the Lord whisper our name. The Twenty-third Psalm does not say "though I walk through the *valley of death* thou art with me." It says, "though I walk through *the valley of the shadow of death* thou art with me." The shadow of a mean grizzly bear cannot attack you. It can only scare you if you let it. Think of it. Jesus walked through the valley of death so that you and I will never have to. The Word tells us that we will go through the flood, but we shall not be overtaken. We shall go through the fire, but not be consumed (Isaiah 43:2). After the testing of our faith, we shall come forth as gold (Job 23:10). God has not promised believers that our lives will be like skipping through a beautiful park, eating grapes and cherries without problems or challenges. Jesus said, "In this world, you will have tribulation, but to fear not, for I have overcome the world."

There is hope and safety in the middle of a dark valley because Jesus walks with us. He goes before us. He is the waymaker, and he has promised to be our rearguard. Isaiah 52:12 says, "The Lord will go before you; the God of Israel will be your rearguard." The Lord has us covered on all sides. The late Tommy Thompson once said that he didn't mind walking through the valley, "because that is where the lilies grow." Jesus is called the lily of the valley or the bright and morning star, and he is the fairest of ten thousand. Some of you reading this teaching may be thinking that I am being presumptuous and that I don't know what you have been through, your situation, or how badly you are hurting. This is true, but I know a man who does; his name is Jesus Christ. Some of you may have gone through heart-wrenching trials and losses that were so painful, if it had not been for the Lord walking beside you, you would have lost your mind.

The Word tells us that Jesus has suffered in all things. He has suffered and gone through everything that you and I will ever experience. Jesus Christ was all God, and he was all man. He was not half man and half God. Christ experienced rejection, betrayal, hunger, the loss of a dear friend, torture, and death, even the death of the cross. For you who have been rejected by a parent, Jesus knows your pain. Jesus was even rejected by his heavenly Father when he became sin on the cross. We are told in 2 Corinthians 5:21, "For He [God] made Him to be sin for us, who knew no sin; that we might be made the righteousness of God in Him." At Calvary, Jesus Christ became the scapegoat for all mankind. There was a moment, while he hung on the cross, that Jesus, who knew no sin, became sin. All our sins were placed on him. When Jesus became sin, his heavenly Father could not look on him, and he turned away from Jesus. When God turned his back on his son, Jesus felt the sudden separation from his father. He knew he was alone. He had been abandoned, and he was experiencing the weight of the sin of the whole world on himself. This caused the humanity of Christ to cry out, "Eli, Eli, lema sabachthanni, My God, My God, why have you forsaken me?" (Matthew

27:46). It is important to recall that through Christ's life, he always referred to God as his heavenly Father except when he became sin on the cross. At that moment, Jesus did not call God father but called him "My God, My God." God could no longer look on Jesus, and he turned away and let him die alone. The only time God has ever turned his back on a person who cried out for help was with his own son. Our heavenly Father gave up his only Son so that he could rescue you and me (John 3:16).

It is difficult to really understand why God loved us so much, but he did and still does. When Jesus slumped and died, his spirit returned to the hands of God, his body went to the grave, and his soul descended into the lower parts of the earth (Ephesians 4:9). And three days later, Jesus rose from the grave. He did all that by faith, not as a super angel but as a man. Jesus called himself the Son of Man seventy-seven times. Jesus overcame it *all!* This is why he can be our high priest in heaven, our advocate, ever making intercession for us. To everyone who has been forsaken by a parent or someone they love, Jesus understands. He is here to heal your emotional bruising; he knows what it is like to be forsaken.

Jesus is the firstborn of many brethren to them who believe and confess him as their Savior. As adopted children of God, we will never experience our heavenly Father turning his back on us. He will never leave or abandon his children because of what Jesus did for us at Calvary. Jesus endured separation from his heavenly Father so that we never will. A dear friend of mine, Pastor Jim Ayars, said recently, "Believing in Jesus Christ makes us fireproof." In other words, the flames of hell can never touch us, because the blood of Jesus has cleansed us from all unrighteousness.

St. Paul often used Roman customs or laws to illustrate a spiritual truth. Under Roman law, a father could have a public ceremony when his son turned a certain age and could declare publicly that he was adopting his son. This declaration by the father had significant and legally binding consequences. After announcing he had adopted his own son, the father could never disown or disinherit his now adopted son, regardless of what happened in the future. This is the security that we have as adopted spiritual children through Jesus

Christ. Our heavenly Father will never disinherit us or throw us out of his heavenly family. We have been adopted by God himself when we believed in his son, and we are in the family of God forever.

Intercession, a Powerful Tool of Prayer

The dictionary defines intercession as an act of praying in behalf of another. This is an oversimplification of intercessory prayer. Many books have been written about intercessory prayer, what is it, and how does a person operate in it. I will not attempt to discuss intercession in detail here. I will only illustrate the results of intercessory prayer when it is used to protect and help others. The book of Ezekiel 22:30–31 gives us some understanding of how it works and why it is a necessary part of our prayer life. God said in Ezekiel 22, "I looked for a man among them to make a hedge and stand in the gap before me for the land, …but I found none." What a sad indictment against Israel. Ezekiel tells us what and why God wanted an intercessor for Israel. Intercessory prayer can and will protect a person's life and can even save a nation. In Ezekiel's time, the Israelites had fallen into whoredom and idolatry. Because of their rebellion and whoredom, God considered them dross, which is worthless residue that remains after metals have been purified. God said he would even burn up the dross, meaning his judgment would be complete. Ezekiel prophesied both before and after the destruction of Jerusalem. God did not want his people to be destroyed and taken captive to Babylon. So God looked for someone to stand in the gap and build a hedge of protection so his people would not be destroyed, but found no one.

I have always been amazed that the Jewish people, after experiencing mighty miracles and protection from God, would turn to idols (more than once) instead of Yahweh for worship and prayer.

They had to know that idols can't hear; they don't have ears! In Ezekiel 22:30, God indicated that if he could have found an intercessor in Samaria and Jerusalem, they would have been spared. God wanted a man to stand in the gap that had been created by Israel's idolatry and rebellion, a person who could turn the wave of sin away from God's people and bring them to repentance. Protection for God's people could have been accomplished through intercessory prayer. Today God still desires and looks for believers who will stand in the gap and build a hedge so that our nation will not be destroyed.

God, throughout the centuries, has placed a hedge of protection and blessing around his people. When Israel turned to whoredom and idolatry, a breach or opening occurred in the hedge that surrounded God's people, and a tsunami of wickedness flooded into God's camp. The Israelites were taken captive because they turned away from God and because they were whoring after the heathens and became polluted with their idols (verse 30). Even after all of Israel's sin and alienation from God, he still desired to save Israel.

An example of intercession is found in Genesis 18, where Abraham interceded for all the righteous people in Sodom. Abraham began his intercession before God by asking, "If he [Abraham] found fifty righteous people in Sodom, would God spare the city for the sake of the fifty righteous?" God answered yes. Abraham continued his earnest requests until he finally got down to asking, "If ten righteous were found in Sodom, would God spare the city?" God said, "I will not destroy it for [the] ten's sake." I believe if Abraham would have asked God one more time, "If I can find four righteous in the city, will you spare the city for the sake of the four"? I believe God would have said, "Yes. I will spare Sodom for the sake of the four righteous." We know that after Abraham and Lot's family left Sodom, it was totally destroyed.

What we are to glean from these stories is that God can be touched with intercessory prayer and even withhold judgment. In Exodus 32:9–14, while Moses was visiting with God on the mountain, God revealed to Moses that the children of Israel had made a golden calf and were worshipping the idol and making sacrifices. God grew angry and told Moses to stand aside so his wrath could wax hot against them. God wanted to consume them because of their evil, but Moses interceded for the Israelites, asking God to spare the people (verse 11–13). The Lord, in verse 14, changed his mind and did not destroy them.

In part, this is what my grandma Elizabeth did for Eddie Hopkins, my father. She earnestly interceded for him, standing in the gap and making up a hedge of protection around my dad, so that he would not be destroyed before he could make Jesus Lord of his life.

Intercession for the Saints

Intercession is the act of praying in behalf of another. Have you ever been going about your day when suddenly you had an overwhelming need to pray for a friend or a family member? Maybe you didn't even know that they were in need of prayer for healing or protection, but a sense of urgency to pray for them swept over you. That was the Holy Spirit prompting you to intervene in prayer in behalf of another. The person you are interceding for may not even know that they are in danger or are headed for disaster. Before I share stories and testimonies on how intercession has preserved ministries and protected individuals, I want to introduce someone to you.

Her name is Marie Dobrinski. I met Marie and her husband, Lester, in Phoenix, Arizona, many years ago at my ordination service. It was customary after a person was ordained to preach a sermon. After I spoke, a long line of people formed to shake my hand; and after about thirty minutes, as the line shortened, I noticed an elderly couple at the end of the line. As they drew closer, I noticed the lady had apparently forgotten to wear her false teeth. She was moving her jaw back and forth in a chewing motion, and at times, her chin almost touched her nose. As she got closer to me, I began to notice something other than her missing teeth. I began to feel the presence of the Lord, and I realized this lady had a special anointing on her life. When she took my hand, I almost fell over backward. Her anointing was so strong and dynamic emotion swept over me. Marie told me about the pain and rejection I had experienced as a child and as an adult. She blessed my ministry and prophesied that God would open up doors to many denominations where I would preach the gospel of grace. Marie cautioned me that I would face Satan's attacks in the future and that I would become a target, but to fear not, for the Lord had protected me from birth and that he would always be beside me. Marie was absolutely correct in her ministry to me that day. After a few months, I realized the Lord had sent a wonderful gift—a prayer warrior. Marie Dobrinski put us on her prayer list to pray not only that our ministry would be effective but also that our lives would be protected. Marie later informed me that the Lord had impressed on her to be our intercessor. After many decades, I believe God is still honoring her prayers of blessing and protection.

For several years, we traveled the country, singing and preaching, often being on the road for five or six weeks at a time. When we would come home to Phoenix after a long road trip, I would go to Lester and Marie's home the next day to share the spiritual victories we had experienced on that tour. After one of those long tours, I went to visit Marie. After inviting me in, with an excited tone, Marie declared, "On Wednesday night, August 16, you were slated for death by the devil. What happened?" I had to think back a few days to remember where we were ministering at that time. After a few moments of reflection, I recalled that we had been singing in a church in Des Moines, Iowa, that Wednesday night. The concert was over, and while Denny and I were loading our equipment into the coach, I noticed a tall young man walking toward me on the sidewalk. As he got closer, I noticed the young man's bizarre behavior. While he walked, he made gesturing motions with both of his hands as though he was swatting bugs. I sensed potential danger, so I instinctively put my back (leaned) against the coach and waited for him to pass. A few seconds later, Denny Watson, our new guitar player, walked out of the church, carrying equipment. As we loaded the equipment, we heard a woman screaming about fifty feet away. We turned and saw the man who had just walked past me, reaching through an open car window, trying to jerk an elderly lady's purse away from her while striking her in the head with his other hand. Denny and I yelled at the attacker to stop while we ran over to the car to see if the lady was injured. The attacker ran down an alley, and we foolishly pursued the young man. It was at night, and as we approached what looked like a storage building, I announced in a loud voice, "Come out. We just want to talk to you!" The attacker came out of hiding with a revolver in his hand pointed right at us. Denny and I raced back to the church, and as I entered the church, I shouted for everyone to take cover and that there was a man outside with a gun. The pastor then called the police. The elderly lady was not seriously hurt and only sustained two or three bruises.

After sharing the above story with Marie, she told me what happened on Wednesday morning, August 16, while she and Lester were fishing on a lake. While they were trolling in their boat, Marie suddenly turned to Lester and said, "Get me back to shore. Gary is in trouble; he has been slated for death." When they got back to shore, Marie and Lester got into their camping trailer, and Marie began praying. She prayed for hours, mostly groaning, in the Spirit until she felt a breakthrough and had peace.

Marie, through intercessory prayer, stood in the gap for us and built up a hedge of protection so Satan could not destroy Denny and me. Because of Marie's sensitivity to the prompting of the Holy Spirit to intercede, we escaped not only serious injury that night but also possibly death.

Someday when we are in the Lord's new kingdom, Jesus himself will present rewards to believers, and guess who will be in the front lines? Intercessors, like Marie Dobrinski, who have been in the shadows and who have spent years interceding daily for men and women who were laboring in the ministry. The intercessors will no longer be in the background but will be front and center when awards are handed out in heaven. To me, these prayer warriors are the real spiritual heroes. A prayer warrior is a believer who battles against spiritual forces (Ephesians 6:12) by interceding for others, not only to protect them but also their ministry will bring people to the saving knowledge of Jesus Christ. When you see someone's ministry or a church growing with many new believers, it is neither because of a beautiful building with fancy doors nor because the preacher is good-looking and an eloquent speaker. It is because people have been earnestly praying and interceding and breaking down spiritual walls in behalf of that ministry.

St. Paul constantly asked the churches to remember him in prayer because Paul knew that supplications and intercessions defeated the hindering forces of hell here on earth. God has provided believers with a host of spiritual weapons, which are gifts, and when we use them, they work every time. I must admit, before meeting Marie, I had limited knowledge, if any, about the prayer of intercession and vicarious faith and how they worked. It is easier to share the victorious results of intercessory prayers than it is to teach how it works and how to develop the ministry of an intercessor. Becoming an anointed intercessory prayer warrior is a special calling. It can be time-consuming and can open you up to attacks from the devil. But fear not, for greater is he who is within you than he who is in the world.

I am going to share several more situations where intercessory prayer brought deliverance and salvation to individuals and to a city. I was invited to speak in a church in Fremont, California, for eight nights. After four nights of speaking, I was becoming weary. During the first four nights, I felt as though my words were coming out of my mouth and falling to the floor in front of me. As I looked out to the audience, it was as though I was looking at over two hundred dead people sitting straight up, staring at me. Nothing was happening spiritually. I even thought maybe we should load up our equipment and leave town.

On Thursday morning, I called Marie Dobrinski for prayer. Marie began to earnestly pray, and within minutes, she made these observations: Marie stated, "I see a church that is long and wide with a high ceiling and wooden beams near the ceiling going from left to right."

I said, "Marie, that describes it perfectly."

She continued, "Gary, there are selfish fat demons sitting on those wooden beams, looking down at you, laughing while you are preaching. They are hindering the anointing and the flow of the Holy Spirit." Marie then operated in the authority as a believer and commanded those disruptive demons to get out of that church and not to return in the name of Jesus Christ!

I knew, after Marie's prayer, the service on Thursday night was going to be special. From the opening song to the alter call, the people responded with praise to God and worshipped the Lord with thanksgiving. I now knew that I could build up their faith with the Word of God and prepare them for the healing service on the last night. There were many people in that church suffering with depression and physical sickness; I knew the Lord wanted to touch and heal them. On the last night of the meetings, the people were ready to receive from the Lord. The spiritual table of blessing was set through intercessory prayer and the Word of God.

After the sermon, there was a beautiful time of prayer with the people at the altar. The pastor asked me to pray for his twenty-two-year-old daughter, who was suffering with rheumatoid arthritis and had difficulty functioning in her daily activities. The pastor's daughter was not in the service that night. So several believers gathered around the pastor and his wife; we laid hands on them and prayed the prayer of faith for their daughter, believing for her healing, in the name of Jesus.

A friend of mine, who attended the Fremont Church, called me about one year later and gave me an update on the pastor's daughter. This young woman had been told by her doctor that she may end up in a wheelchair as she aged and that she would never be able to have children. My friend reported that she not only had nearly all the arthritic symptoms disappeared but also had married and would soon deliver her first baby. All praise and glory to the one who created us. These miracles happen when we pray according to God's Word and when we pray by believing we have received. Hallelujah! Praise the living God.

I will share one more situation that illustrates how the prayer of intercession can break Satan's grip and control over a city. Many years ago, I was asked to speak in a Native American missionary church in Gallup, New Mexico. On the second day of our visit, I decided to visit downtown Gallup and buy some necessities. What I saw in the streets of Gallup was shocking and concerning. The town was dirty and dilapidated, and there were people passed out on the sidewalk and in the alleys. While walking on the sidewalk, I heard a sound behind me. I turned to look, and there was a drunk driver in a pickup truck, driving on the sidewalk. The pastor informed me that every night, at least one Native American would be found dead from an overdose or from alcohol poisoning. My heart began to break for the plight of these Native Americans who were suffering physically and spiritually. My meetings ended, and I returned to Phoenix with a heavy heart.

About one year later, a pastor from the Pentecostal Church in Gallup asked me to speak for several nights in his church. I arrived on a Sunday, and as I looked around, I could see Gallup had not changed. On Monday morning, I felt led to spend time in prayer for the people of Gallup. I drove north of town where there were hills with large boulders. I climbed to the highest point where I could see all of Gallup, and I began to pray. I felt righteous anger toward the devil for what he had done to these precious Native Americans. I prayed for a revival to sweep across this community and prophesied that Satan's grip would be broken and asked God to send a messenger to this city in Jesus's name. I wasn't the only person praying for healing and deliverance over this community. Many Christians and small missions had been laboring for years to bring the good news to these people.

That night, as I began to speak, a young Native American man entered the church and walked all the way up to the platform and grabbed my left arm. In a diabolical animal-like low voice, he said, "I'm going to get you, baby. I'm going to get you." I asked the elders to please escort that young man to a prayer room and minister to him. I returned to my sermon, and after the altar service, I visited the young man in the prayer room. He was very docile and quiet. I ministered grace to him and let him know that Jesus loved him and so did I.

The next morning, I had an early lunch with the pastor, and he informed me that all hell broke loose in town overnight. He said there were stabbings and acts of violence many times worse than normal. This report reminded me of what happened after we prayed deliverance over my dad four years earlier. After our prayer of deliverance for my dad, he became belligerent and hateful and experienced loss of memory and greatly increased his vodka consumption.

If you recall his story in part 1, I mentioned that after the prayer of deliverance, my dad's drinking increased to a level that would have poisoned most people, but deliverance and salvation eventually came forth. When believers operate in the Word of God and take authority over Satan in the name of Jesus Christ, the devil must go, whether you are interceding for one person or for a city. Through these experiences, I came to understand why the prayer of intercession is so important and what to expect after you have prayed for a person's deliverance from satanic control. When believers operate under the anointing and command Satan to release someone in the name of Jesus, there is often a tearing or ripping as the evil spirits leave that person or town. I believe this is what happened with my dad and in Gallup, New Mexico. I wasn't the only believer interceding for that town. Obviously, the evil spirits became very upset when they were commanded to leave Gallup, even to the point where they sent a young man to the church that night to harm me. I had apparently made the devil very angry.

I did not return to Gallup for many years. About fifteen years ago, I was talking to a pastor friend, and I mentioned my experience in Gallup and the pathetic conditions the Native Americans were experiencing. My friend stated, "Haven't you heard about Gallup?" I said no. He proceeded to share that Gallup had experienced a spiritual revival. He said an evangelist with a large tent held revival meetings for several weeks in Gallup. He thought it was evangelist Cerullo or possibly another tent evangelist from Pennsylvania. My friend said that hundreds of people were delivered from alcohol and saved. He stated that Gallup was completely changed. That evangelist was the messenger who brought the message of grace to the people in Gallup. All glory and praise to our heavenly Father who is faithful to honor the prayers and intercessions of his children.

I had the opportunity to visit Gallup about twelve years ago with my son Tim. As we entered Gallup, I could hardly believe what I saw; I did not recognize the town. No longer were people passed out on the walkways or in the alleys, and nobody was driving their trucks on the sidewalks. The town had had a makeover spiritually and physically. There was new life and vitality in Gallup. I cannot take any credit for the revival that took place in that city. I only prayed for those people as the Holy Spirit directed. There were a host of prayer warriors (believers, evangelists, pastors) who interceded in prayer, for years, until revival swept through that area. It took a team of believers to save that village.

Vicarious Faith

A Tool of Prayer

Previously, I discussed the importance of intercessory prayer and how it can build a hedge of protection around an individual and a ministry. Intercession is to intervene in behalf of another. There is another tool in our spiritual prayer arsenal that is a partner to intercessory prayer. When we pray vicariously for someone, we are totally concentrating and involved in the need(s) of that individual. Vicarious prayer is acting for another or experiencing the feelings of another person. Vicarious faith is beyond having empathy for a person who is suffering mentally or physically. When you vicariously pray for another, you will often experience the physical pain that that individual is suffering.

I was discussing vicarious faith with my prayer warrior, Marie Dobrinski, when she shared a story that helped me understand how vicarious prayer works. There was a lady in one of the churches in Phoenix who had been diagnosed with stomach cancer. She was in her thirties, was married, and had children. She was experiencing a lot of pain and nausea and could only eat very little. The family asked Marie to put this cancer-stricken lady on her prayer list. Marie put everything on hold (shopping, cooking, and socializing) so she could fully dedicate her time in prayer for this sick lady. Marie shared that she began to pray with her understanding; then she prayed in the spirit with groaning that could not be uttered or explained.

The dictionary defines the word *groaning* as "a deep inarticulate sound conveying pain and heavily laden with travail." In Romans 8:26, Paul said, "But the Spirit itself maketh intercession for us with groanings which cannot be uttered." As Marie prayed in the Spirit, she suddenly incurred agonizing pain in her stomach. Nausea and weakness overcame her as she ministered in intercessory prayer for the sick and dying lady. Marie said that when the symptoms of cancer pain attacked her, she then knew how badly this lady had been suffering. The intensity of the pain became so great that Marie asked her husband to call the church and ask believers to pray that the Lord would give her strength to continue interceding for this lady. For two days, Marie experienced the pain and nausea as she interceded in prayer. She could not eat and could only drink very little water. After two days suddenly, the pain and nausea left, and Marie knew that the spirit of infirmity that had attacked this lady was broken. Friends, I am not making this up; it is the Bible. Paul admonished us in Galations 6:2, "Bear ye one another's burdens, and so fulfil the law." After about two weeks, Marie received a wonderful report from the lady who was sick with cancer. When she returned to her oncologist, another CAT scan was performed to check the status of the tumors. Her doctor was shocked and amazed. The tumors were gone, and there was no trace of cancer! All praise and thanksgiving to our Father in heaven.

After gaining some knowledge of intercession and how vicarious faith works, I asked the Lord to help me become more sensitive to the pain of others so that I could know the depth of pain that people were experiencing. We were scheduled to minister in a small church in Cheyenne, Oklahoma, for several nights. We stayed with a couple who had a beautiful ranch where they raised cattle and quarter horses. Bob Burroughs and his wife owned the ranch, and they were a friendly and loving couple. While staying with them, Bob told us of a tragic event that had happened four years earlier. His five-year-old grandson was visiting for a few days, and Bob decided to take his grandson for a ride on his quarter horse. It had been raining, and the ground was very wet and slippery. Bob had his grandson sitting on the saddle in front of him, and as the horse started to gallop, the horse's feet slipped out from under him. The horse rolled over, and the saddle horn crushed the little boy's chest. He died in seconds. A family member who was there at the time of the accident saw Bob walk onto the porch and enter the house, carrying the limp body of his grandson.

As Bob shared that story, he didn't show any emotion. Bob simply spoke in a soft, low voice as he recalled the accident. He did share that the death of his grandson emotionally devastated the family for a long time. I got the impression that Bob and his family had been able to work through the loss of the little boy. It appeared they had accepted the death and had moved on with their lives. I could not have been more wrong.

On the last night of the meetings, I invited people who wanted prayer to come forward. There were about fifteen people in line, and Bob was at the end. As I got about four feet from Bob, I began to have a sharp, crushing pain in my chest, and I thought, *Oh Lord, please don't let me have a heart attack here at the altar. I'm trying to minister to these people.* The chest pain did not let up. In fact, the closer I got to Bob, the more intense the pain became. When I took his hand to pray with him, I could hardly breathe. I then realized the Lord was letting me experience the literal heartache that Bob had lived with since the death of his grandson. In that prayer line, God healed Bob of the guilt, the shame, and the heartache he had carried with him for over four years. Grief and extreme heartache can shorten a person's life.

After the service, Bob shared with me that since the death of his grandson, his health had been declining. In the four years since the accident, he developed heart trouble, high blood pressure, and weight loss; and he had lost interest in doing things he previously enjoyed. I kept in touch with Bob for several years after the prayer at that altar, and Bob reported that his health had been fully restored—no more heart problems and no more high blood pressure. The heartache and depression he had lived with were gone. He had regained his vitality, and the joy of his salvation had returned. Blessed be the name of the Lord.

The Holy Spirit

Our Prayer Partner

There are times when we do not know how to pray in a given situation. But God has provided to us a prayer partner who assists us in our prayer life and who helps us to pray according to the will of God. Paul stated in Romans 8:26–27, "Likewise the Spirit also helpeth our infirmities: for we know not what we should pray for as we ought: but, the Spirit itself maketh intercession for us with groanings which cannot be uttered. And he that searcheth the hearts knoweth what is the mind of the Spirit, because he maketh intercession for the saints according to the will of God." In other words, the Holy Spirit knows the mind of God; and when we don't know what to pray for in our own understanding, the Holy Spirit prays through us with groanings, which cannot be expressed in our known language. Paul said in 1 Corinthians 14:15, "I will pray with the Spirit and I will pray with the understanding also: I will sing with the spirit and I will sing with the understanding also." The Holy Spirit is with us to help us pray accurately and in the will of God. When the Holy Spirit prays through us, he will never pray outside the will of God. What a wonderful gift our heavenly Father has given us—praying in the Spirit. Not only does the Holy Spirit pray for us and through us, but when we pray in the Spirit, the devil cannot understand one word of that prayer. Paul told us to run a good race, to finish the course. As we run the spiritual race in this world, we are not alone. Jesus said the Holy Spirit is within you and will always be with you

(John 14:16–26). The Holy Spirit is our Paraclete, which means he runs beside us, encouraging us and telling us we can finish the race. He says, "Don't give up and don't quit. You are going to make it. You are almost there. I'm right here with you." The devil can only rob us of our blessings if we decide not to fight the good fight of faith.

I Will Get the "Tip"

There have been many times I have shared a meal in a restaurant when a friend picked up the bill to treat me, and I said, "Oh, I'll get the tip." This made me think about the marriage supper we will have with our Lord in heaven. That supper will be completely paid for by our Lord, and we will not have to leave a tip. Why? Because Jesus paid for it all at Calvary. Many Christians find it difficult to believe that salvation is a gift. When Jesus found us, we were in spiritual grave clothes ready for hell; but he rescued us, loosened those death rags, and set us free. When we accepted Christ as our Savior, we stepped out of those grave clothes and into a new reality. That new reality was to become a new creature in Christ; we were then born into the family of God.

When we are born again, we become part of a new bloodline. We then have the spiritual DNA of God within us because of Christ's precious, incorruptible blood. We are saved by grace through faith, not by our works, lest any person boasts. I have had conversations with friends over the years regarding eternal life. I always share that I am saved to the uttermost and that Jesus is able to keep me until I stand before him. But sadly, many Christians believe that you can love and serve the Lord all your life but still lose your salvation if you have a bad thought or commit a bad act just before dying. Believing that you will not know if you are saved until after you die is eternal insecurity.

The church I was raised in taught that kind of false doctrine. They did not believe that the finished work Jesus performed at Calvary was enough; they had to contribute or add something to their salvation. They needed to leave a "tip." That kind of doctrine kept me from completely embracing Jesus as friend and Lord. Spiritual insecurity will keep you from having peace and a close, intimate relationship with Jesus Christ. If you can't trust Jesus to keep his promises to you concerning being sealed in him by the Holy Spirit for eternity, a love-and-trust relationship will not come to fruition. Our salvation and eternal life are because of Christ's obedience to his Father and of his blood sacrifice on the cross. Salvation is not of ourselves; it is all about him. You don't have to leave a "tip." He has it all covered! Jesus paid for all our eternal debt. He has forgiven us of a whole life of sin. How could I not love and serve him? What Jesus wants from us is to be close to him, to rely on him, to put our faith and trust in him, and to reflect his character of unconditional love to others.

Final Thought

Prayer and Faith

Revelation tells us that all the prayers of the saints are held in censers in the throne room of God. A censer is a container in which incense is burned during a religious ceremony. In Revelation 5:8, we are told that the prayers of the saints fill golden vials with odors, which are our prayers. Revelation 8:3–5 says, "And another angel came having a golden censer; and there was given unto him much incense, that he should offer it with the prayers of all saints upon the golden altar, which was before the throne. And the smoke of the incense, with the prayers of the saints, ascended up before God out of the angel's hand." Our prayers do not have an expiration date.

The above scriptures reassure us that God does not throw out or discard our prayers but keeps and preserves them in golden censers close to him in heaven. In God's timing (verse 5), all the prayers that were put forth in faith and in accordance with God's will will be answered. Then Revelation 8:5 states, "And the angel took the censer and filled it with fire of the altar, and cast it into the earth." I believe verse 5 not only speaks of God's judgment coming to earth, resulting from the saints' prayers, but also illustrates how God answers prayer at the right place and in the right moment to release the answer to our petitions. Our prayers continue to be safely held in the presence of God and his Son.

This is what God did with Grandma Elizabeth's intercessory prayers for my dad, Eddie. God held her prayers in his golden censers in heaven until Eddie was in the right place and was ready to accept Jesus as his Lord and Savior. Grandma Elizabeth died twenty-seven years before Eddie's deliverance and salvation experience.

There are two more scripture verses I want to leave with you. Again, I want to assure all believers that when you pray to the Father in the name of Jesus Christ and pray in his will, God hears your requests; and in his timing, he will grant you your petitions. Jesus assured us in John 15:17, "Since you abide in me and my words abide in you, you shall ask what you will, and it shall be done unto you." Have you made Jesus Christ Lord of your life? If yes, then you abide in him, and his words abide in you. Even in the Old Testament, God assures us that he hears our prayers. In Psalm 34, God promises, "For the eyes of the Lord are upon the righteous, and his ears attend to their prayers." If you are born again, then you are righteous in the sight of God, and this promise is yours. In Jeremiah 1:12, God promises, "For I am watching over my word to perform it."

Almost all Christians, at some point in their lives, have suffered from a faith-deficit disorder. Don't be hard on yourself. Be encouraged. The scriptures tell us, "Line upon line, precept upon precept, He is changing me." If I have made anyone feel that their faith is inadequate, that was not my intention. It often takes an evangelist to jolt us out of our comfort zone. Our faith is increasing daily as we walk with the Lord. It is a process that continues all our lives until we see Jesus face-to-face.

My life has been enriched while spending months researching and organizing the scriptures to bring you this teaching. May it bring faith, hope, and blessing into your life. My prayer is that the writings in this book have not only given you hope regarding the salvation of your family members but that God's word has also helped you stretch and increase your faith. I now realize I was not just writing this book for you but was also writing it for myself. I also need to constantly hear the scriptures regarding faith, grace, and the power of prayer. If you ever feel discouraged or feel your prayers are not being heard, please review the scriptures in this book regarding faith and prayer. Developing the God kind of faith is a lifetime journey.

Because of a prayer warrior's intercession for my dad and of God's faithfulness to hear and answer our prayers, my father will someday greet me at heaven's door, and he will say, "Gary, welcome home."

Closing Prayer

I feel in my heart that many of you who have finished reading this book may have never accepted Jesus Christ as your personal Savior. I want to pray with you. There is hope in the midst of your darkness. There is a place for you at God's table of grace. Please don't harden your heart to the Gospel of Salvation. This is your moment to accept Jesus Christ as Savior and receive eternal life. Jesus has been waiting for you all this time. Jesus came to bring light to those who are in spiritual darkness and are living in the shadow of death. Jesus wants to give you peace and life everlasting. Please pray this prayer with me:

> "Father in heaven, bring your light into my darkness. Deliver me from the things that have controlled me. I accept Jesus Christ as my Lord and Savior. Thank you for hearing my prayer and accepting me into your heavenly family. I ask this in the name of Jesus Christ."

If you prayed that prayer, 2 Corinthians 5:17 declares that you are a new creature (person) in Christ Jesus. You now belong to a holy family and have a home in heaven forever. The following is now your statement of faith in Jesus Christ:

> "Jesus, I believe and confess that you lived for me and died for me on a cross and that you went to the lower parts of hell for me, rose from the dead for me, and ascended into heaven for

me; and now you are my Savior, advocate, and high priest in heaven. Amen."

Carry this with you and read it aloud every day. I encourage you to find Christian fellowship where you can continue to grow in the knowledge of Jesus Christ and in his grace that he has provided for you and for all mankind. Be Blessed.

Eddie Hopkins

Eddie Hopkins with his son Gary

Eddie's Bible

About the Author

The author, Gary Edward Hopkins, was born in Iowa on a farm, and when he was fifteen years old, his family moved to southern California. There he finished his academics, earning a degree in business and later a Juris Doctor degree. He was ordained into the ministry in 1974 and pastored two churches during the next three decades. Gary also formed a singing group called the Chapel Trio that sang part-time for thirty-nine years.

Gary has five sons and one daughter, and he resides in Rochester, Minnesota, with his wife, Linda. They enjoy traveling and singing gospel music together. Gary continues to write about the endless love, grace, and mercy of God that have come to all mankind through and by Jesus Christ.

CPSIA information can be obtained
at www.ICGtesting.com
Printed in the USA
LVHW030129101021
700033LV00001B/8

9 781098 097561